Ridiculously BIG KIDS' JOKE BOOK

The biggest, most exciting collection of witty, weird, wonderful and hopelessly corny jokes that you will absolutely love to bits!

Collected and Illustrated by

Peter Coupe

ARCTURUS

Published by Arcturus Publishing Limited
for Bookmart
Desford Rd
Enderby
Leicester
LE9 5AD

This edition published 2000

Printed and bound in Finland

©Peter Coupe / Arcturus Publishing Limited

ISBN 1 - 84193 - 033 - 4

Ridiculously BIG

KIDS' JOKE BOOK

Contents...

School Screams

Teacher - Blenkinsop - Give me a sentence with the word detention in it !

Blenkinsop - I had to leave the horror film before it had finished, because I couldn't stand detention !

What do you call someone who greets you
at the school door every morning?

Matt!

★

Head – Why haven't you been in school for the last
  two weeks?

Pupil – It's not my fault – whenever I get to
  the road outside the school I'm never
  allowed to cross!

Head – Why aren't you allowed to cross?

**Pupil – Because there is a man with a sign saying
  'STOP CHILDREN CROSSING!'**

Fred - YUK! These school dinners taste of soap!

Freda - Well, at least you know the kitchens are clean!

Where would you find giant snails...?

...at the end of giant's fingers !

5 good reasons to go to school...

1   Even school dinners are better than my dad's.

2   The heating goes off at home at 9 o'clock.

3   You learn to be independent -
     by doing as you're told!

4   The video shop doesn't open 'til 4 o'clock!

5   You learn what life will be like when you are old
     and grumpy - by watching the teachers at
     coffee break.

Blenkinsop - Sir, my parents want me to tell you that
they were really pleased with my last report.

Teacher -   But I said you were a
complete idiot ?

Blenkinsop - But it's the first time
anyone in our family has been
really good at something!

Head - What do think about in the school holidays ?

Pupil - I never think about schoolwork !

Head - Not really much of a change for you then ?

Head - Mr Snurge, why have you put the school orchestra into the school freezer ?

Mr Snurge - They said they wanted to play some music that was a little more cool !?

For tonight's homework I want you to write an essay on a goldfish.

I can't do that Sir !

Why on earth not ?

I don't have any waterproof ink !

I'm not really interested in maths - I just go along to the lesson to make up the numbers!

Teacher -   Name a bird that doesn't build its own nest.

Blenkinsop - The Cuckoo.

Teacher -   That' right - how on earth did you know that?

Blenkinsop - Everyone knows that Cuckoos live in clocks!

★

Did you hear about...

The P.E. teacher who used to run round the exam room in the hope of jogging pupils memories ?

The maths teacher and **the art teacher** who used to go out together painting by numbers ?

The craft teacher who used to have the class in stitches ?

The science teacher who was scared of little glass dishes - he was petrified ?

The cookery teacher who thought Hamlet was an omelette served with bacon ?

Why did the school canteen hire a dentist ?

To make more filling meals !

★

I banged my head on my locker door this morning !

Have you seen the school nurse ?

No, just stars !

★

Head - Why were you sent out of the tennis class today ?

Pupil - For making a racket !

What exams do farmyard animals take ?

Hay levels !

Teacher - Blenkinsop , If
five cats were on
a bus and one gets off,
how many would be left ?

Blenkinsop - None, sir !

Teacher - How do you get
that answer ?

**Blenkinsop - Because the
other 4 were copycats !**

★

Teacher - Who can tell me
which sea creature eats its
prey two at a time ?

Pupil - Noah's Shark !

Which of Shakespeare's plays was
about a bacon factory?

Hamlet!

What's the difference between a
bird watcher and a teenager?

One gets a hide and spots, the other
gets a spot and hides!

Why is
Frankenstein's
monster rubbish
at school?

He hasn't got
the brains he
was born with!

Teacher - Smith, what were people wearing during the Great Fire of London ?

Smith - Blazers, smoking jackets and hose ?

What is a good pet for small children ?

A Rattlesnake ??

Why were ancient sailing ships more eco-friendly ?

Because they could go for hundreds of miles to the galleon !

★

Teacher - Smith, I do wish you would pay a little attention !

Smith - I'm paying as little as I can, sir !

★

Teacher - Did you find the exam questions easy ?

Pupil - Oh, yes I found the question all right, it's the answers I couldn't find !

★

Why does our robot games teacher never get sick ?

Because he has a cast iron constitution !

★

Teacher - Mary, why was no-one able to play cards on Noah's Ark ?

Mary - Because Noah stood on the deck !

Teacher - John, name me a famous religious warrior !

John - Attilla the Nun ?

Teacher - Smith, where are you from ?

Smith - London.

Teacher - Which part ?

Smith - All of me !

Teacher - Did you know that most accidents happen in the kitchen ?

Pupil - Yes, but we still have to eat them !

Teacher - Who was Thor ?

Pupil - The God who kept Thcratching hith thpot !

How do you cure lockjaw ?

Swallow a key ?

★

Teacher - If you had to multiply 1345 by 678
what would you get ?

Sarah - the wrong answer !

John - Dad, have we got a ladder ?

Dad - What do you need that for ?

John - For homework I have to write
an essay on an elephant !

English Teacher - Did anyone help you
write this poem Carol ?

Carol - No Miss.

English Teacher - Well, I'm delighted to meet
you at last Mr Shakespeare !

Teacher - Sid - what is a goblet ?

Sid - A baby turkey ?

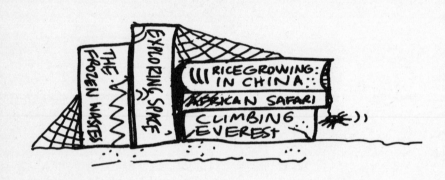

★ NEW BOOKS IN THE GEOGRAPHY LIBRARY ★

RICE GROWING IN CHINA by **Paddy Fields**

AFRICAN SAFARI by **Rhoda Lion**

EXPLORING SPACE by **Honor Rocket**

THE FROZEN WASTES by **S. Keemo**

CLIMBING EVEREST by **Percy Veerance**

ANIMAL SCHOOL REPORTS...

Cheetah - A nice enough boy, but not to be trusted.

Leopard - Has missed a lot of classes
this year due to spots.

Hyena - Seems to think that everything is a joke.

Stick Insect - Never been the same since the elephant
mistook him for a pencil!

Teacher - Steven, name an ancient musical instrument.

Steven - An Anglo - saxophone ?

Teacher - Jim, what is the largest species of mouse in the World ?

Jim - The Hippo pota - mouse !

Teacher - Sarah, what evidence is there that smoking is harmful to the health ?

Sarah - Well, just look what happened to all the dragons !

Teacher - Smith, why is the handwriting in your homework book exactly the same as Blenkinsop's ?

Smith - I borrowed his pen ?!

Why did the boy throw his wristwatch out
of the window in the history exam ?

He wanted to make time fly !

Teacher - Why were you late for school today Carol ?

Carol - I got a flat tyre on my bicycle !

Teacher - Did you run over some broken glass ?

Carol - No, sir, there was a fork in the road !

Head - I want you all to be aware of the
importance of punctuality !

**Blenkinsop - Well, I should be alright, I get
good marks in English !**

Teacher - Steven, what's a computer byte ?

Steven - I didn't even know they had teeth !

Head - Have you any idea how many teachers
work at this school ?

Pupil - About a quarter of them it seems to me !

Teacher - Why were you late this morning Veronica ?

Veronica - I squeezed the toothpaste too hard, and
it took me half an hour to get it all back
into the tube again !

★

You have a photographic memory Blenkinsop,
it's a shame that nothing ever develops !

★

Teacher - Jarvis, tell me a sentence with the
word counterfeit in it.

Jarvis - I wasn't sure if she was a centipede or
a millipede so I had to count her feet !

Computer Teacher - Smith, give me an
example of software.

Smith - A floppy hat ?

Teacher - How would you stop a cockerel waking you at 5 a.m. ?

Pupil - Eat him for supper before you go to bed !

The Deputy Head is a funny chap,
who creeps from class to class,
he has a face that could curdle cream
and a voice like broken glass !

Teacher - Blenkinsop, How would you discover what life in Ancient Egypt was really like ?

Blenkinsop - I'd ask my Mummy !

What's the difference between a school
and a headmaster's car ?

One breaks up, the other breaks down !

Teacher - What's the difference between a
horse and an elephant ?

Pupil - A horse doesn't look like an elephant !

A bottle of lemonade went to teacher training college
what subject was he going to teach ?

Fizzical education !

A butterfly went to teacher training college -
what subject was she going to teach ?

Moth - a - matics !

Teacher - Who discovered Pluto ?

Pupil - Walt Disney ?

Pupil - Ugh! There's a fly in my soup !

**Kitchen assistant - Don't worry, the spider
on your bread will get it !**

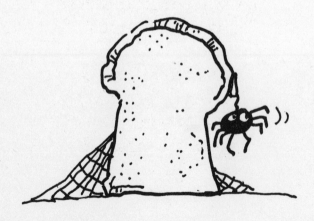

★

Blenkinsop , what do birds eat for their breakfast ?

Tweet - a - bix ?!

Did you hear about the music teacher who kept
forgetting her register !?

We love our school
We really do
We love our lessons
Teachers too!

We love the exams
and the tricky tests
We love the school dinners
and the P.E. vests !

But why do I sound
so cheerful today
Because we just started
the Summer holiday !!

Teacher - Have you been an idiot all your life ?

Pupil - No, not yet !

What do you call the German teacher who
goes to school on a motor bike ?

Helmut !

Why are teachers like doctors ?

Because they are both good at examinations !

English Teacher - Sally, do you like Kipling ?

Sally - I don't know, Sir, I've never eaten one !

My last school was so rough they didn't have a school photograph - they sent home identikit pictures instead !

Science Teacher - Gary, do you know what Copper Nitrate is ?

Gary - Yes Sir, it's what they pay policemen on night duty !

History Teacher - Martin, where would I find Hadrian's wall ?

Martin - Wherever Hadrian left it, Sir !

Teacher - name one of Noah's children.

Pupil - Joan of Arc ?

And... for all those who were late this morning because they stayed up to watch the football... we're going to make School more like football...

you will all stay behind and do extra time tonight as a penalty !

Maths teacher - Blenkinsop, can you tell me the 9 times table please ?

Blenkinsop - You asked me that yesterday, don't tell me you've forgotten it already !

Where do Martians go to train to be teachers ?

Mooniversity !

Teacher - You're on English level 4 aren't you, Smith?

Smith - Yes.

Teacher - Then take this English level 2 book for your father or he's never going to be able to catch up and do your homework properly !

★

I think my maths teacher is in love with me...

How do you work that out ?

...she puts red kisses all over my homework !

★

What's the best snake to take into a maths lesson ?

An adder !

I would have done my homework, but.....

I didn't have any pocket money left, and my sister always demands cash in advance.....

My dad was working late, and he has all the brains in the family.....

My pen ran out and I spent all night looking for an inkwell.....

What is a history teacher's favourite fruit ?

Dates !

Please Miss, is it true that the French only ever eat one egg for breakfast ?

What makes you ask that ?

Because yesterday you said that in France, one egg is un oeuf !

Did you hear about the teacher who had to wear sunglasses in the classroom?

He had extremely bright pupils!

Anxious parent - What do you think my son will be when he has finished all his exams?

***Teacher* - An old age pensioner!**

How many teachers does it take to work the photocopier?

Who cares, as long as it keeps them out of the classroom!

Why do swimming teachers like elephants ?

Because they never forget their trunks !

*We've got a new drama teacher -
she's a real class act !*

Head - That's Hodgkiss, the school bully.

Visitor - How dreadful, can't you do anything to stop
him ?

Head - Certainly not, or I'd never get the teachers
back to the classrooms after lunch break !

Who is a teacher's
favourite actor ?

Michael Caine !

Our cookery teacher knows his onions...

Our P.E. teacher thinks we're a real shower...

Our last maths teacher was taken away...

**Our music teacher never accepts notes
from home...**

Where do new teachers come from ?

They're produced on an assembly line !

What were the names of the very
first teachers ?

Miss and Sir !

Teacher - Is your father helping you with your
homework ?

Pupil - No, sir, if anything he knows even less than I do !

Teacher - Smith, give me a sentence with the word politics in it.

Smith - My pet parrot swallowed the alarm clock and now Polly ticks !

What's the best way to tell your maths teacher that you have forgotten to do your homework - again ?

From a great distance !

Teacher - If your father gave you £1.50 pocket money and your mother gave you £2.50, what would you have ?

Pupil - Someone else's parents !

Teacher - Well, at least I know that no-one in the school football team will ever start smoking.

Head - How do you work that out ?

Teacher - Because they always lose their matches !

Our School cook was arrested for cruelty - she was caught beating eggs, battering fish fingers and whipping cream !

John - I bet our chemistry teacher could cure your insomnia mum...

Mum - Why, is he a doctor as well ?

John - No, but as soon as he starts to speak half the class fall asleep !

Teacher - Are you sending Gary to boarding school ?

Parent - Yes. His report says he is always bored !

Teacher - How many letters in the alphabet ?

Pupil - 25 !

Teacher - How do you work that out ?

Pupil - Well, it's Christmas next week, so there's Noel !

Head - Why did you call Mulder and Scully into the school ?

Pupil - I looked into the school kitchen and saw an unidentified frying object !

Teacher - Jenkins, what's the difference between an elephant and my desk ?

Jenkins - Don't know sir.

Teacher - In that case I think I'll send someone else to put these books in my desk drawers !

Teacher - I just don't understand how one person can make so many mistakes in their homework !

Pupil - Oh I can't take all the credit, sir, my Dad did most of it !

We sent our teacher's photograph to a lonely hearts club...

They sent it straight back - they said they weren't THAT lonely !

How can you tell when a teacher is in a good mood ?

No, I don't know either !

What do you call a teacher with a pile of sports equipment on his head ?

Jim !

What do maths teachers do when their
sinks get blocked?

They work it out with a pencil!

★

What do cannibals have for school dinners?

Snake and pygmy pie, with chimps and beings!

★

What do you call a boy who only just
gets to school on time every day?

Justin!

★

*Did you hear about
the maths teacher
who wanted an
Italian take away, but
was divided about
whether to have
additional cheese!*

Our technology teacher left to try and make something of himself !

Who's your favourite teacher ?

The Finnish one !

We haven't got any Finnish teachers !

Yes we have. Every day she says "Finish what you're doing and go home !

Mum - How did you do at school today ?

John - Great ! The teacher told me I was a moron !

Mum -And it's not as if you come from a religious family !

Well, son, how did you find the maths exam ?

Unfortunately, it wasn't lost !

Teacher -
Blenkinsop. Can you tell me the 9 times table ? !

Blenkinsop -
If you don't know it at your age,
what chance have I got !

★

What do you get if you cross a teacher and a
traffic warden ?

Someone who gives you 500 double yellow
lines for being late !

Games Teacher - Read these books and
they will help you get fit
- they are exercise books !

Johnny –
Hey, Dad, I'll bet you can't write in the dark !

Dad –
Of course I can !

Johnny –
Good! I'll just turn out the light
and you can sign my school report !

Of course in my day we didn't have
computers to help us...................

...........we had to get our schoolwork
wrong all on our own !

I think Johnny will make an excellent astronaut when he
leaves school...

Why do you think that ?

...because he's had nothing but space
between his ears all the years he's
been at this school !

I would have done my homework, but.....

I used up all the ink in my pen
drawing the curtains.....

they didn't have any more copies of Romeo and Juliet in
the video library.....

you said to hand it in tomorrow - and I will.....

★

What is an English teacher's
favourite fruit ?

The Grapes of Wrath !

★

Please Miss, is it true that in the future all trains and buses will run on time ?

What makes you ask that ?

Because my dad says that they will still run on petrol !

Did you hear about the cross eyed teacher who had to retire ?

He couldn't control his pupils !

He must have been related to the one-eyed teacher who also had to retire...

...because he didn't have enough pupils

★

Head -
I understand you're interested
in a career in languages ?

Pupil -
Yes, sir, my English teacher says
I speak perfect gobledygook!

★

Why are maths teachers good at solving detective
stories ?

Because they can tell when all the clues add up !

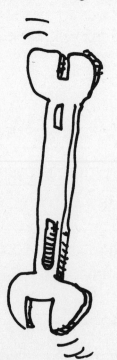

★

We have a new Italian teacher
-
I'll bet she pasta lot of exams
to get this job !

★

What is a robot teacher's
favourite part of the day ?

Assembly !

Why did you give an apple to our exchange werewolf teacher from Transylvania ?

Because I wanted to be creature's pet !

★

Our cookery teacher **grills** anyone who fails to hand in their homework...

Our P.E. teacher thinks we're all **good sports**...

Our maths teacher gives us **additional** homework...

Our music teacher makes a real **song and dance** when we're late for class...

★

Where do vampire teachers come from ?

Teacher Draining College !

Where do vampire teachers like to work ?

In the school necks door !

Your son is so dim, he doesn't even know where Hadrian's Wall is !

Well, if Hadrian lost it what has that got to do with our Cedric !

What's the easiest way to get a day off school ?

Wait until Saturday !!

Steve - I wish MY dad would help me with my homework like yours does !

Joe - I wish your dad would help me as well. I got 3 out of 25 and another detention thanks to mine !

Pupil -
Do I need any
qualifications to
work as a vet?

Careers teacher -
No, you've had plenty of experience with animals
already - I've seen the rest of your class!

Teacher -
The school cook has been caught soaking
the eggs in whisky again!

Head -
What on earth was she doing that for?

Teacher -
Because she wanted to serve scotch eggs!

I think you've been built upside down Blenkinsop!
Why do you think that sir?
Because your feet smell and your nose runs!!

Teacher -
Your son is rather troublesome in class, did he go to a good school before he started here ?

Parent -
Oh Yes, it was approved !

★

Teacher - Why are you taking those trainers into your exam ?

Pupil - I'm hoping to jog my memory !

★

Teacher - How many letters in the alphabet ?

Pupil - 11 !

Teacher - How do you work that out ?

Pupil - t - h - e - a - l - p - h - a - b - e - t !

★

Teacher - Jenkins, what's the difference between a fairy story and the excuses you give me for not doing your maths homework ?

Jenkins - Don't know sir.

Teacher - A fairy story is believable !

They tell me that my schooldays
will be the happiest of my life,
but they haven't met the matron here, the cook or the
headmaster's wife !

Here's your
chemistry exam
paper Blenkinsop -
totally unhurt !

What do you mean
totally unhurt ?

I mean there's not
a mark on it !!

What do you call a teacher
with a pile of bricks
on his head ?

The Housemaster !

Why can you always believe
what a teacher
with a beard tells you ?

They can't tell bare faced lies !

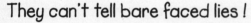

**That new monster teacher is terrible - Jim was late
yesterday and he bit his head off !**

I saw *my* history teacher in
town last night...
...he was out on a date !
...his girlfriend is a
history teacher as well...
**...they go to a restaurant
and talk about old times !!**

Did you hear about the Spanish teacher
looking for a job -

she castanet far and wide !

Glory, glory alleluyah
teacher hit me with a ruler
the ruler broke in two and
so she hit me with her shoe
and I wish I was at home...

★

Blenkinsop - what's the
easiest way to make a fire
using two sticks ?

Make sure one of them
is a match, sir !

Carol - when was Rome built ?

Well, it must have been at night because I know
Rome wasn't built in a day !

I want to be a jockey,
what qualifications will I need ?

Three Hay levels !

Our teacher put his sunglasses on when he gave out
our examination results today...

..he took a very dim view of our performance !

★

Smith - how do you make a hot cross bun ?

Pour hot water down a rabbit warren, sir !

Blenkinsop -
why did Robin Hood steal from the rich ?

**Because the poor didn't have anthing
worth stealing !**

How does a maths teacher know how long
she sleeps ?

Because she takes a ruler to bed with her !

Teacher - Be honest, Smith, what do you think this homework is worth ?

Pupil - Well, I paid £3.50 to Steven Blenkinsop for it !?

Did you hear about the cannibal teacher...

All his pupils were all late, and now they're all ate !?

Blenkinsop - what type of musical instrument did the early Britons play ?

The Anglo Saxophone ?

When our science teacher retired we bought her a bottle of toilet water - it cost £15 !

What !? You could have had some water from our toilet and I would only have charged you £2.50 !!

Of course in my day you only had the one choice
for school dinners...................

.............Like it or lump it !

What is the space alien's favourite
school subject ?

Art - because he
likes to create Marsterpieces !

Eric should make an excellent train driver, as he has more experience of lines than any other pupil in the school!

Pupil - Do I need any qualifications to work as a Father Christmas in a department store ?

Careers teacher - You need Ho ! Ho ! Ho ! levels !

What do you call a man with a school on his head ?

Ed !

New pupil -
Who is that over there wearing spurs and a silver star and carrying a saddle over his shoulder ?

Old pupil -
Oh! That's the Deputy Head !

Maths Teacher - Carol, why have you brought a picture of Henry the eighth in with you ?

Carol - You told us to bring a ruler in with us today !

Teacher - Smith, give me a sentence with the word indifferent in it !

Smith -
My television doesn't work anymore since I plugged the aerial indifferent !

Head - You boy, stop running around like that ! Don't you know who I am ?

Pupil - There's a bloke here who doesn't even know who he is !

★

Teacher -
If you had 50p in each trouser pocket, and £1 in each blazer pocket what would you have ?

Pupil - **Someone else's uniform !**

John - We've started a school fencing team !

Mum - Do you need any equipment ?

John - **A paintbrush and some creosote !**

Why do robot teachers never get scared ?

Because they have nerves of steel !

Why are you taking the Queen into your exams ?

It's a maths exam, she's my ruler !

Crazy Names

What do you call a man with
very strong spectacles?

Seymore!

What do you call a man
with a sack, a long
white beard and a
sleigh?

**Bjorn, the oldest
postman in Iceland!**

What do you call a monkey who is King of the jungle?

Henry the Ape!

What do you call a woman with a shotgun in her hand?

Whatever she tells you to, or else!

What do you call a woman who laughs as
she drives her car?

Minnie Ha Ha!

★

What do you call a glove puppet
that sweeps chimneys ?

Sooty !

★

What name do you give a dog
that likes to wander off all the time ?

Rover !

What do you call a man
who owns a seaside
sweet factory ?

Rock !

★

What do you call a
woman with a frog on her head ?

Lily !

What do you call a man who lives in Scotland?

Glen!

What do you call the Roman Emperor who kept pet mice?

Julius Cheeser!

What do you call a man with a horse's head?

Nathan!

What do you call a woman who sells parrots?

Polly!

What do you call a woman who was eaten
by her cannibal husband ?

Henrietta !

What was the name of the man who designed King
Arthur's round table ?

Sir Cumference !

What do you call a man with a
car number plate on his head ?

Reg !

What do you call a man with his head in the oven ?

Stew !

What do you call an Ancient Egyptian
with no teeth ?

A Gummy Mummy !

What do you call a man with a tissue paper head ?

Russell !

What do you call a man with a
speedometer
on his head ?

Miles !

What do you call a failed lion tamer?

Claude Bottom!

★

What do you call a frightened man?

Hugo First!

★

What do you call a man with
a bowl of
porridge on his head?

Scott!

What do you call a man with
an oil well on his head?

Derek!

What do you call a girl with a bag of chips ?

Anita !

What do you call a woman with
a plant pot on her head ?

Rose !

What do you call a man who lifts
cars up in a garage ?

Jack !

What do you call a woman
who keeps horses ?

GiGi !

What do you call a woman who only comes out
at Christmas ?

Carol !

What do you call a man who dances with
bells round his ankles ?

Maurice !

What do you call a woman with a
cash register on her head ?

Tilly !

What do you call a dog that is a always
rushing about ?

A dash-hound !

What do you call a rodent that likes to sword fence ?

A Mouseketeer !

What do you call a man who delivers
Christmas presents to lions and tigers ?

Santa Claws !

What do you call a man who doesn't sink ?

Bob !

What do you call a woman who knows
where she lives ?

Olivia !

★

What do you call the super heroes
who got run over ?

Flatman and Ribbon !

What do you call the illness that martial
arts experts catch ?

Kung Flu !

What do you call a man with a
computer on his head ?

Mac !

What do you call a man with a
duck on his head ?

Donald !

What do you call a woman who
works at the zoo ?

Ellie Fant !

What do you call a man with
horses on his head ?

Jim Karna !

What do you call a woman with a ball of
wool on her head ?

Barbara Black Sheep !

What did the Spaniard call his first
and only son ?

Juan !

What do you call a man with a vaulting horse on his
head ?

Jim !

What do you call a girl who
comes out
very early in the morning ?

Dawn !

What do you call a girl with
cakes on her head ?

Bunty !

What do you call a man with money on his head ?

Bill !

What do you call a boy with an
arm and a leg on his head ?

Hand - toe - knee !

What do you call a man with a small pig on his head?

Hamlet!

What do you call a woman who plays snooker with a pint of beer on her head?

Beatrix Potter!

What do you call a man with a male cat on his head?

Tom!

What do you call a man with
a castle on his head ?

Fort William !

What do you call a man with a box of
treasure on his head ?

Chester !

What do you call a woman with a
sinking ship on her head ?

Mandy Lifeboats !

What do you call a woman with a
pyramid on her head ?

Mummy !

What do you call a man with a
police car on his head ?

Nick, nick, nick...!

★

What do you call a man with a wooden head ?

Edward !

★

What do you call a woman with
two toilets on her head ?

Lulu !

What do you call a girl with a
head made of sugar ?

Candy !

What do you call a girl with
a head made of glass ?

Crystal !

What do you call a girl with a
head made of honey ?

Bee - trix !

What do you call a man with
legal documents on his head ?

Will !

What do you call a man with a
jumbo jet parked on his head ?

Ron Way !

What do you call a man with a steering wheel and
gearstick on his head ?

Morris !

And what do you call his son ?

Morris Minor !

What do you call a woman with
a boat tied up to her head ?

Maude !

What do you call a woman with a
tub of butter on her head?

Marge!

★

What do you call a lion with toothache?

Rory!

★

What do you call a man with an
anvil on his head?

Smith!

What do you call a man with a
heavy goods vehicle on his head ?

Laurie !

★

What do you call a dog that's
always snapping at people ?

Camera !

What do you call a criminal with
a fish down his trousers?

The Codfather!

What do you call a girl with an
orange on her head?

Clementine!

What do you call a girl with a bucket
and spade on her head?

Sandy!

What do you call a girl with a chimney
on her head ?

Ruth !

What do you call a man with
a pile of hay on his head ?

Rick !

What do you call a man with
turf on his head ?

Pete !

What do you call a man with a school
register on his head ?

Mark !

What do you call a girl with
flowers growing out
of her head ?

Daisy !

(The girl with the beauty
spot!)

★

What do you call a man with a
vegetable patch
on his head ?

Mr Bean !

What do you call a woman with a
badly fitted head ?

Lucy !

What do you call a play acted by ghosts ?

A Phantomime !

★

What do you call a Scottish lunchtime assistant ?

Dinner Ken !

★

What do you call the ghost that
haunts TV chat shows ?

The Phantom of the Oprah !

What do you call a man with a
road map on his head ?

Miles !

What do you call a woman with a kettle on her head ?

Polly !
(well, in the nursery rhyme
Polly put the kettle on ?!)

★

What do you call a man with a pair of
spectacles on his head ?

Luke !

What do you call a woman with a
doll on her head ?

Sindy !

What do you call a man with a
sprig of holly on his head ?

Buddy !

What do you call a man with a large
fiery planet on his head ?

Sunny !

What do you call a woman with some
thin paper and a pencil on her head ?

Tracey !

What do you call a woman with
half a lizard on her head?

Liz!

What do you call a man with a used
postage stamp on his head?

Frank!

What do you call a man with a policeman on his head?

Bobby!

What do you call a woman with a plate of
food on her head?

Amelia!

What do you call a vampire with
a calculator on his head ?

The Count !

What do you call a man with some
cheese on his head ?

Gordon Zola !

What do you call a man with a
bear on his head ?

Teddy !

What do you call a woman with a
steering wheel on her head ?

Carmen !

What do you call a teacher with
a joke book on his head ?

A Tee-Hee-Cher !

What do you call a man with a
pile of chopped firewood on his head ?

Axel !

What do you call a man with
a mortgage offer stapled to
his head ?

The Loan Arranger !

What do you call an overweight vampire ?

Draculard !

What do you call a man with a cable
coming out of his ear ?

Mike !

What do you call a man who does
everything at top speed ?

Max !

What do you call a man who fills himself
with fried slices of potato and makes a
noise in the cinema ?

Chris Packet !

What do you call a super hero who
looks after books ?

Conan the Librarian !

What do you call a woman who works
for a solicitor ?

Sue !

★

What do you call a man who goes fishing
every weekend ?

Rod !

★

What do you call a teacher
with earplugs in ?

Anything you like - he can't
hear you !

★

What do you call a man who keeps
pet rabbits ?

Warren !

★

What do you call a man and woman who show you up in front of your friends ?

Mum and Dad !

★

What do you call a man who likes drawing and painting ?

Art !

★

What do you call a man who does odd jobs and lives just round the corner ?

Andy !

★

Prisoner - It's not my fault. I was given a name that was bound to lead me into crime !

Judge - *What is your name ?*

Prisoner - **Robin Banks !**

What do you call a woman who
hates butter ?

Marge !

★

What do you call a 35 stone sumo
wrestler ?

Whatever he tells you to !

★

What's the name of that really
strict teacher

Miss Norder - Laura Norder !

★

What do you call a
man with seagulls
on his head ?

Cliff !

★

What do you call a masked man who
lends you money ?

The Loan Arranger !

What do you call a woman who checks
punctuation ?

Dot !

Did you hear about
the man who used
to make his living
selling refreshments
in the interval at
football matches ?

His name.......... Alf Time !

99

What do you call a
Scotsman with his own
computer ?

Mac !

★

What do you call a man
who keeps pet
rabbits and writes
epic novels ?

Warren Peace !

★

What do you call a man
who keeps an angry
ferret down
his pants ?

Very, very stupid !

★

What do you call the man who stamps the letters at the Post Office ?

Frank !

★

What do you call a man who works in a perfume shop at Christmas ?

Frank in Scents !

★

What do you call a Spanish woman having a meal in a restaurant ?

Juanita !

★

If you really loved me, You'd let me call you Jack. Then you could lift my car and mend the puncture at the back !

What do you call a girl who has her own car ?

Minnie !

★

Is it true... that the man who invented the toilet was called...

...Lou ?

★

What do you call someone with more money than sense ?

My best Pal !

★

What do you call a woman who has a boat tied up at the riverside ?

Maude !

What do you call a man with loads of money ?

Rich !

What do you call a fish that tunes pianos ?

A Piano Tuna !

What do you call Mr Smith's half brother ?

Arthur Smith !

What do you call a magician's assistant ?

Trixie !

What do you call someone who never blows his nose ?

Ronnie !

What do you call a man who likes to grow flowers, fruit and vegetables ?

Gordon !

What do you call the brother and sister who like to build things across rivers ?

Archie and Bridget !

What do you call a girl who likes to cook in the garden ?

Barbie !

What do you call a woman with a food processor on her head ?

Belinda !

What do you call someone who claps when contestants get the right answer ?

Santapplause !

What do you call the camel with three humps that fell off the wall and smashed into millions of pieces ?

Humphrey Dumpty !

What do you call a man who lies in front of your door all day ?

Matt !

What do you call a girl with lots of suitcases ?

Carrie !

★

What do you call cattle thieves who wear tissue paper trousers ?

Rustlers !

★

That frog is a secret agent - his name's Pond,

James Pond !

★

What do you call a man who slowly runs out of energy ?

Peter !

★

What do you call
a girl who lives in
a pond ?

Lily !

What do you call
a nun with a radio
on her head ?

A Transister !

What do you call
a teacher who
eats toffees in
class ?

A Chew-tor !

What do you call the man who carries a football
team from one match to another ?

The coach !

What do you call someone that witches go to when they are sick ?

A witch doctor, of course !

★

What do you call an Eskimo's house if it doesn't have a toilet ?

An Ig !

★

What do you call a house in France with two toilets ?

Toulouse !

★

What do you call it when a toilet is closed and bricked up ?

Loo - brick - ation !

What do you call a teacher who has a
lot of accidents ?

Miss Hap !

What do you call the hairstyle you get from
sticking your head in an oven ?

A Micro - wave !

What was the name of the explorer with a
passion for biscuits ?

Captain Cookie !

What do you call the boy who is also a goat ?

Billy !

What do you call
someone who gets paid
to go to college ?

Grant !

What do you call a cat
that eats lemons ?

A Sourpuss !

What do you call a
chicken that eats
cement ?

A Bricklayer !

What do you call the
ghost of a Star Trek
character ?

Doctor Spook !

What do you call a loud
mouthed soccer fan ?

A foot bawler !

What do you call a jogger
in a safari park ?

Fast food !

What do you call the
box a toad keeps
his tools in ?

A Toadstool box !

What do you call a
ghosts favourite
TV soap ?

Horror Nation Street !

What do you call an
executioner's
favourite TV programme ?

Noose at ten !

What do you call a cricketer
who only
plays at night ?

The Star player !

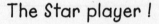

What do you call 36 inches when you're in
Glasgow ?

A Scotland Yard !

What do you call the pudding that fought at the battle of the Little Big Horn ?

General Custard !

What do you call a parrot
when he has dried off after
a heavy rainstorm ?

Polly Unsaturated !

What do you call a man
that people sit on in meetings ?

The Chairman !

What do you call a vicar
on a Honda 750
motorbike ?

The Rev, rev, rev !

What do you call the place where spooks go for their holidays ?

A Ghost House !

What do you call a cake that is exactly the same as another cake ?

A Carbun copy !

What do you call a miniature version of one of the Beatles ?

Small McCartney !

★

What do you call a
computer's favourite
cake ingredient ?

Electric currents !

★

What do you call a
woman who
lets you
borrow money ?

G-Lenda !

★

What do you call a
man made up of
spare body parts ?

Hand Toe Knee !

★

What do you call a bear that plays
with Prince Charles ?

A Polo Bear !

What do you call a
ghost who picks his
nose ?

A Bogeyman !

What do you call
a young bee ?

A Baby !

What do you call a
bee with feathers ?

A Buzzard !

Which famous battle
did bees fight in ?

Battle of Hastings !

★

What do you call a bee with his own car ?

A Bee-M-W !

★

Is it true...

that the man who invented ice came from...

...Cuba ?

★

What do you call your brother's smelly son ?

My ne-phew !

What do you call a
Scottish android ?

Robot the Bruce !

★

What do you call a man
with three legs ?

Nothing - he's certain
to catch you if
you do !

★

What do you call the steak and kidney
pudding that hit an iceberg ?

The Pietanic !

What do you call someone
who talks to his
houseplants ?

Potty !

What do you call a glass
robot ?

See - Through - P - O !

A garage owner called his first daughter Toyah,
then he called his second daughter
Toyah as well...

She was the spare Toyah !

What do you call
a Roman emperor
who has
adventures ?

An action Nero !

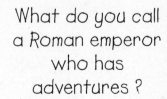

What do you call the
detective who catches
underwear thieves ?

Nick. R. Lastic !

What do you call a
radio presenter who
plays records in
alphabetical order ?

An A. B. C. D. J !

What do you call a
man who only
eats casseroles ?

Stu !

What do you call a
Russian gardener ?

Ivanhoe !

What do you call
the woman who
fell off the white
cliffs ?

Eileen Dover !

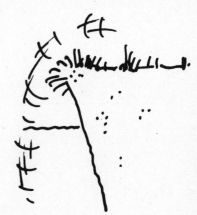

★

What do you call a girl with
her own sweet shop ?

Candy !

★

What would
you
call a band
that
your father
joined ?

A Pop Group !

★

What do you call a man who dances in coal mines
with hankies in his hands ?

A Morris Minor !

What do you call a girl who
lives under the house ?

Cella !

What do you call
a girl who lives
in a jar ?

Jamima !

What do you call a
teacher who
falls asleep in
the class ?

Nothing! You don't
want to wake him up !!

★

What do you call a chicken
that lays lightbulbs ?

A battery hen !

★

What does the invisible man
call his *mum* and *dad* ?

Transparents !

★

What was Humpty Dumpty
wearing the last time
you saw him ?

A Shell Suit !

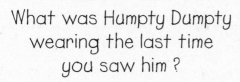

What do you call a dead parrot ?

A Polygon !

★

What do you call an animal that eats weeds ?

Dan de Lion !

★

What do you call a ghost's horse ?

A Nightmare !

★

What do you call a
dangerous woman
who works in a
cake shop ?

Tilly the bun !

★

What do you call a man with a cactus
on his head ?

Sandy !

★

What do you call a man with a wooden leg and a
steak and kidney pudding on his shoulder ?

A Pierate !

★

What do you call a Roman emperor
with a mouse on his head ?

Julius Cheeser !

What do you call a
skeleton that
refuses to
do any work ?

Bone Idle !

What do you call a woman who sneezes all the time and likes knock, knock jokes?

Tish who ?!

What do you call a woman with a crown on her head?

Your Majesty !

Awesome Animals

What sort of music do you hear most in the jungle?

Snake, rattle and roll!

On Christmas Eve a married couple were looking up into the sky at something travelling towards them.

Is it a snow storm ? asked the wife

No, it looks like reindeer, replied the husband.

What do you do if an elephant sits in front of you at the cinema ?

Miss the film !

What did the Pink Panther say when he stood on an ant ?

Dead ant, dead ant, dead ant dead ant dead ant...

What do elephants take to help them sleep ?

Trunkquilisers !

Where do tadpoles change into frogs ?

In the croakroom !

What did the dog say when it sat on some sandpaper ?

Ruff !

What do you call a delinquent octopus ?

A crazy, mixed -up squid !

What is the most cowardly farmyard creature ?

The Chicken !

What is the cheapest way to hire a horse ?

Stand it on four bricks !

What is the tallest yellow flower in the World ?

A Giraffodil !

What sort of bird steals from banks ?

A Robin !

What is green and white and hops ?

An escaping frog sandwich !

Why is an elephant like a teacher ?

Put a tack on an elephants chair
and you'll soon find out !

★

What do you call a stupid elephant with his
own aeroplane ?

A Dumbo Jet !

★

Mary had a little lamb
the lamb began to tease her
'Stop it', she said,; the lamb refused
and now it's in the freezer !

★

When Mary had a little lamb
the doctor was surprised
but when old MacDonald had a farm
he couldn't believe his eyes !

Why did the chicken blush ?

Because it saw the salad dressing !

What sort of animal does a ghost ride ?

A night mare !

How do ducks play tennis ?

With a quacket !

What do you get if you cross a hunting dog with a
newspaper writer ?

A newshound !

★

What do you call a large grey animal that's
just eaten a ton of beans ?

A smellyphant !

★

Why do bears have fur coats ?

Because they can't get plastic macs in their size !

Where is the hottest place in the jungle ?

Under a gorilla !

Two cows were talking in a field....

First Cow - Are you worried about catching this mad cow disease ?

Second Cow - Baaaa !

What is big and grey and good at sums ?

An elephant with a calculator !

Why did the chicken run out onto the football pitch ?

Because the referee whistled for a fowl !

Where do horses sit when they go to the theatre ?

In the stalls !

Why did the chicken cross the playground ?

To get to the other slide !

What ballet stars pigs ?

Swine Lake !

What do you do with a green elephant ?

Wait until he's ripe !

Why don't elephants eat penguins ?

They can't get the wrappers off !

What do sheep use to get clean ?

A Baaaa of soap !

What happened to the frog's car when it broke down?

It was toad away!

★

What do you get if you cross a
crazy dog and a sheep?

Baaaarrking mad!

★

Which is the trendy horse?

The one with the pony tail!

What says Moo, Baaa, Woof, Quack, Meeooow, Oink ?

A sheep that speaks foreign languages !

Which animals with a cold do the police use ?

Sniffer dogs !

Where would you find a martian
milking a cow ?

In the milky way !

What is the best way to get in touch with a fish ?

Drop him a line !

Good morning Mr Butcher - do you have pigs' trotters ?

No, I always walk like this !

What do you get if you cross a pig with a millipede ?

Bacon with legs !

Where do rabbits learn to fly helicopters ?

In the hare force !

Why can't I get the King of the jungle
on the telephone ?

Because the lion is busy !

What was the name of the woman who crossed the
Gobi desert on a dromedary ?

Rhoda Camel !

★

Why does a Flamingo lift up one leg ?

Because if it lifted them both up it would fall down !

What grows down as it grows up ?

A Goose !

Where would you hear fowl language on a farm ?

Outside the chicken coop !

My mum and dad said my new boyfriend isn't fit to live with pigs !

What did you say to that ?

I stuck up for him, I said of course he is !

★

Why do elephants have trunks?

Because they would never fit their huge clothes into a suitcase!

★

When do lions have twelve feet?

When there are three of them!

★

First leopard - **Hey, is that a jogger over there?**

Second leopard - **Yes, great, I love fast food!**

★

143

Johnny - Mum, is our dog metric ?

Mum - Why do you ask ?

Johnny - Because Dad said it has just had a litre of puppies ?!

★

What is round, brown, smelly and plays music ?

A cowpat on a record player !

★

When do you know you have chicken pox ?

When you are constantly feeling peckish !

What is black and white and gets
complaints from all the neighbours ?

A Zebra learning to play the drums !

How can you get eggs without chickens ?

By keeping geese and ducks !

Why should you be naughty if you have
a cow for a teacher ?

**Because if you are good you might
get a pat on the head !**

I've lost my dog !!

Why don't you put a card in the post office window ?

Don't be stupid - he can't read !

What do schools of mackerel do before an exam ?

Re - fish - ion !

Where do cows go for their holidays ?

Moo York

or

Patagonia

or

Uddersfield !

Who cuts a sheep's hair ?

The Baaarber !

★

Where do farm animals keep their savings ?

In a Piggy bank !

★

What is it called when a cat falls from the farmhouse
roof and smashes all the glass in the greenhouse ?

A Catastrophe !

★

First goldfish –   I told you we'd be famous one day –
                     and now it's going to come true !

Second goldfish –   Wow! When is all this going
                     to happen ?

First goldfish –   They're putting us on the television
                     tomorrow !

What do you call an insect that has
forgotten the words ?

A Humbug !

Why do octopuses never get mugged ?

Because they are always well armed !

What do pussy cats read with their mice crispies ?

Mewspapers !

If spiders live in Crawley and bees live in Hastings,
where do hares live ?

On your head !

What did the idiot call his pet zebra ?

Spot !

How do frogs send messages to each other ?

Morse Toad !

What game do skunks play ?

Ping Pong !

What was the first motorised vegetable called ?

The Horseless Cabbage !

I'd like a pair of gloves for my dog, please.

What breed is he ?

A Boxer !

What do cows eat for breakfast ?

Moosli !

Why are cows rubbish at maths?

Because they haven't invented the cowculator yet!

What television channel do wasps watch?

The Beee Beee Ceee!

Why do some animals wear cowboy boots in the jungle?

Because they go lion dancing!

Where are all the aspirins in the jungle?

There aren't any - the paracetamol!

What was the 30 metre tall Monopoly box
doing in the jungle?

It was a big game hunter!

What do country and western singers
wear in the jungle?

Rhino-stones!

What is the first thing Tarzan puts on in the morning ?

His jungle pants !

What were Tarzan's last words ?

Who put grease on this vine ?!

Why don't leopards bother to cheat in exams ?

Because they know that they will always be spotted !

★

Why was the zebra put in charge of the jungle army ?

Because he had the most stripes !

What is smelly and has no sense of humour ?

A dead hyena !

What do you call a well dressed jungle cat ?

A dandy lion !

Where does a horse stay on holiday ?

In the bridle suite !

What is cold, furry and minty ?

A Polo Bear !

Where would you find a 10,000 year old cow ?

In a Moooseum !

What sort of sheep stick to the bottom of boats >

Baaaaanacles !

As sheep don't have money, how do they buy and sell ?

They have a baaarter system !

★

Why did the sheep buy a hotel ?

He's always wanted to own a baaa !

★

What sweet thing do sheep like best ?

Chocolate baaaaars !

★

What do cows put on in the morning ?

Udder pants !

How do you control a horse ?

Bit by bit !

Why was the young horse sent out of the classroom ?

He was acting the foal !

Doctor, doctor, I'm turning into a young cat !

You must be kitten me !

What sort of jokes do chickens like best ?

Corny ones !

(which is why we sell so many copies
of this book to chickens !)

Why do cats always finish the job ?

Because they purr - severe !

Where do cats go when they die ?

The Purrr - ly gates !

Where do rodents go for holidays ?

Hamster Dam !

What was the name of the horse that
fought windmills ?

Donkey Oatey !

How can you travel through the jungle at
60 miles an hour ?

Inside a cheetah !

What do Tigers use to wake up in
the morning ?

A Llama clock !

What is the difference between a buffalo and a bison ?

You can't wash your face in a buffalo !

What sort of flowers do monkeys grow ?

Chimp - pansies !

When cows play football, who has the whistle ?

The Heiferee !

Why don't farmers allow sheep to learn karate ?

Because their chops would be too hard !

What do you get if you cross a tortoise with a bird ?

A Turtle dove !

What was the name of the famous French cow painter ?

Too moos Lautrec !

What does a sheep call members of his family ?

Sheepskin !

How do you know when a dog has been naughty ?

It leaves a little poodle on the carpet !

What do you call an electronic dog ?

An Interpet !

Why don't elephants use computers ?

Because they are scared of the mouse !

EEK!

If you give a mouse gorgonzola
cheese what will happen ?

Your computer will smell !

Why did the pony keep coughing ?

He was a little hoarse !

What do sheep do on sunny days ?

Have a baa baa cue !

My daughter took her pet sheep to
the local sports day. '
Is he a good jumper ?,' someone asked her.
'Not yet,' she replied !

Why don't cows sunbathe ?

Because they don't want to tan their hides !

Why did the astronaut jump onto the cow's back ?

He wanted to be the first man on the Moo !

What do they call it when an insect kills itself ?

Insecticide !

What do you get if you cross a baby with a porcupine ?

A lot of problems changing nappies !

Why did the idiot take salt and vinegar to the zoo ?

To put on the chippopotamus !

What do you call an elephant that's also a witch doctor ?

A Mumbo - Jumbo !

Why are elephants such bad dancers ?

Because they have two left feet !

Why do bat mums and dads always
complain about their kids ?

Because all they do is hang around all day !

What did the Boa-constrictor say to the explorer ?

I've got a crush on you !

Which creature builds all the houses in the jungle ?

The Boa-constructor !

What do jungle police officers drive ?

Panda cars !

What did the first Piranha say to the second ?

I've got a bone to pick with you !

Where is it not safe to park in the jungle?

On a double yellow lion!

What do you do if you fancy a bite in the jungle?

Kick a lion up the backside!

★

Which bird is good at chess?

The Rook!

Why is it hard to fool a stick insect ?

Because they always twig !

What are baby stick insects called ?

Twiglets !

Why did the stick insect go to university ?

He wanted to branch out !

★

Two baby skunks - called In and Out - went out for a walk one day. In got lost, but his brother soon found him. How?

In - stinkt !

How would you sell a cow's home ?

You would need to find a byre !

What did the farmer say when the townie asked him if he had any hay ?

Stacks !

What sort of music does a
gifted rodent write ?

Mouseterpieces !

Baby snake - Dad, are we poisonous ?

Dad snake - No, son, why do you ask !

Baby snake - I've just bitten my tongue !

What do they sell at Tarzan's takeaway ?

Finch, Chimps and mushy Bees !

What do you get if you cross a kangaroo with a kilt ?

Hop Scotch !

★

What is a sheep's favourite wine ?

Lambrusco !

★

What do you give a budgie with constipation ?

Chirrup of figs !

★

What kind of fish do pelicans like ?

Any kind - as long as they fit the bill !

What is sheepskin useful for ?

Keeping the sheep's inside where they belong !

What sort of wallpaper do birds like best ?

Flock !

Why do farmers keep cows ?

**Because there are no udder animals
as good at giving milk !**

How do elephants change their car wheels if they have a puncture ?

They lift it up with a jackal !

What bird is always running out of breath ?

The Puffin !

How do you stop a skunk from smelling ?

Tie a knot in his nose !

★

What do you call a goat who robs banks ?

Billy the Kid !

*If a house mouse sleeps in a house
and a field mouse sleeps in a field
do dormice sleep in dorms ?*

Where do rabbits go when they want something
to read ?

Buck Shops !

Rabbit - How do I know this TV will work when I
get it home ?

Shopkeeper -It comes with a full Warrenty !

Name a comedian that dogs really like...

...Ronnie Barker !

Why do elephants paint their toenails red ?

So they can hide in Cherry trees !

Hickory Dickory Dock,
The horse ran up the clock.

Anybody need any firewood ?

Why is the sky so high ?

So birds don't bump their heads !

★

What goes... 'Now you see me, now you don't ?'

A Zebra using a pelican crossing !

What do porcupines eat with their cheese ?

Prickled onions !

★

What do you get
if you cross a
cow with
a camel ?

Lumpy custard !

★

How do you stop rabbits digging up
your garden ?

Easy - take their spades away !

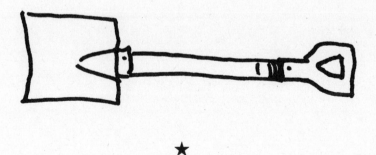

★

We call our dog Blacksmith because every now and again he makes a bolt for the door !

Why are you taking that snake into the maths exam ?

It's an adder !

What do you call an elephant in a telephone box ?

Whatever you like - it will be stuck so it can't chase you !

What goes 'Mark, Mark...'

A dog with a swollen lip !

What are baby crabs called ?

Nippers !

★

*Waiter - Bring me a crocodile
sandwich....
....and make it snappy !*

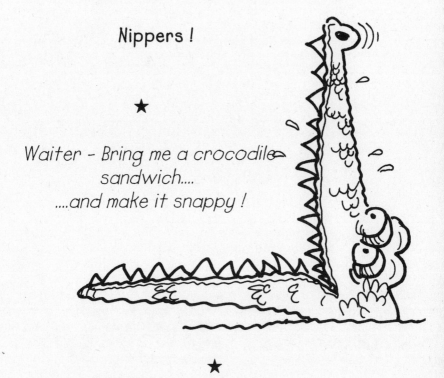

★

Did you hear about the Shetland Pony who
was asked to leave the animal choir ?

She was always a little horse !

★

Why did the hedgehog cross the road ?

He was competing in a point to point race !

What lies at the bottom of the sea and shivers ?

A nervous wreck !

★

What's the fastest fish in the lake ?

A motor Pike !

★

What does your cat eat for breakfast ?

Mine eats Mice Crispies !

★

Did you know that alligators eat beans for breakfast ?

Human Beans of course !

HUMAN BEANS IN TOMATO SAUCE

Noah's Ark was able to find its way about at night because it had been fitted with floodlights !

Why do bees hum ?

Because they have forgotten the words !

Where do you take an injured bee ?

To the waspital !

...just as you would take an injured pony to the horsepital !

What has 10 legs, 3 heads but only 2 arms ?

A man and a dog sitting on a zebra !

What's grey and zooms through the jungle
at 70 miles an hour ?

An elephant on a motor bike !

Why should you never play
cards for money in the jungle ?

**Because there are too
many Cheetahs about !**

What vegetable do you get
if you cross a sheepdog
with a bunch of daffodils ?

A collie - flower !

What game do ponies play ?

Stable tennis !

Why did the hedgehog cross the road ?

He wanted to see his flat mate !

Why did the dinosaur cross the road ?

**Because chickens hadn't been invented
in those days !**

Why did the cat cross
the road ?

**To see his friend
who worked in
the chemists
- Puss in Boots !**

★

Why was the haddock too scared
to use a crossing to cross the road ?

**Because someone told him that
pelicans eat fish !**

Why did the duck cross the road ?

It was the chicken's day off !

Why do elephants have wrinkles ?

Because they hate ironing !

★

What creature comes in handy in the car ?

A windscreen Viper !

Why didn't the young cat get into trouble for telling lies ?

He was only kitten !

What is yellow and very dangerous ?

Shark infested custard !
or
A laser powered banana !

I can't do it, you can't do it, the farmer can't do it...

...what is it ?

Milk chocolate !

★

Another name for parrot food - **pollyfilla !**

★

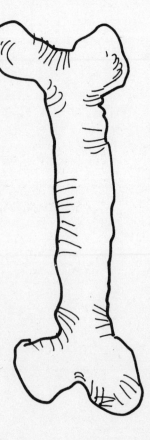

Did you hear about the dog who was too lazy to dig up his bone ?

He was bone idle !

★

How many sheep does it take to make a sweater ?

I didn't even know that sheep could knit !

★

Why does a giraffe have such a long neck ?

Have you ever smelled a giraffe's feet !?

Bullfighting
for
beginners

by

Matt. A. Dores

When sheep are cold they gather in a big circle
and a few sheep in the centre make a lot of
noise and this keeps everyone else warm...

...this is called central bleating !

What do the police have to have before
they can come into your home looking for
escaped parrots ?

A perch warrant !

What does a cat rest his head on in bed ?

A caterpiller !

★

What sort of cat sells wood ?

A Catalogue !

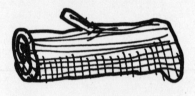

★

What part of a car can be used to change cats into something else ?

The catalytic converter !

★

What bulls hide on the riverbank waiting to charge at you ?

Bullrushes !

★

Which dog is always making mistakes ?

A cock-up spaniel !

What is a cat's favourite TV programme ?

The Mews at Ten !

I'd like a tube of cat glue please !

What on earth is that for ?

Well, I always thought that cats came in one piece - but someone told me you have to buy them as kits !

What was the title of the Shakespeare play about pigs ?

Hamlet !

Why do elephants paint the soles of
their feet yellow ?

So they can hide upside down in custard !

★

**Hickory Dickory Dock,
Three mouse ran up the clock.**

The clock struck one...
...the other two got out of the
way just in time !

★

What is the correct name for a water otter ?

A kettle !

What's green and highly dangerous ?

A frog with a machine gun !

Mary had a little lamb
she also had a horse
for the horse
she made a saddle
for the lamb
she made mint sauce !

Is that budgie expensive ?

No, sir, it's going cheep !

What do you get if you cross
a cow with a child and a pub ?

The milky bar kid !

What is blue and swings through the trees ?

A chimpanzee in a boiler suit !

When is it bad luck to have a
black cat cross your path ?

When you are a mouse !

What is the difference
between an apple and
an elephant ?

Apples are green !

How many elephants does it take to change a lightbulb ?

Four! One to hold the bulb and three to turn the stepladder !

What lives on a ship and says 'croak, croak!' when it's foggy ?

A Froghorn !

What do you call a rich trendy elephant ?
A member of the jumbo jet set !

What do mouse
jokers
like doing best ?

Taking the Mickey !

What do you call a vampire pig ?

Frankenswine !

Did you hear about the 4 elephants who bought a mini so they could play their favourite game... ?

...squash !

How can you possibly be the school swot - you're the least intelligent person I know ?

I know, but I go round killing all the flies !

What do you call a dog that runs up the M1 at 70 miles an hour ?

A two litre Rover !

What is the highest form of
animal life ?

A giraffe !

Have you changed the water in
the goldfish bowl ?

No, they haven't drunk the water
I put in yesterday yet !

What do you call a horse
that sunbathes behind a
venetian blind ?
A zebra !

What do you call a nervous insect ?

A jitterbug !

Why couldn't the butterfly get into the dance ?

Because it was a moth ball !

What is the difference
between a skunk
and a squirrel ?

**Skunks don't know how to
operate a deodorant spray !**

What vegetable do you get if you cross a
sheepdog with a plate of jelly ?

The Collie - wobbles !

What animal do you
eat for pudding ?

Moose !

Name 4 animals from the dog family ...

Mummy dog, daddy dog and two puppies !

Is it true that you can speak
in cat language ?

Me - How ?

Which football team do most
snakes support ?

Slitherpool !

How does a fish teacher
keep control of a
rowdy class ?

**She puts everyone in
their plaice !**

★

Why did the duck cross the
motorway at rush hour ?

I don't know, it must have
been quackers !

★

What is the most
valuable fish ?

The goldfish !

★

What weighs over 1000 kilos and wears
flowers in its hair ?

A Hippy - potamous !

What sort of American holidays
do animals take ?

They fly jumbo jets to Moo York !

★

What is green and very dangerous ?

A 12 bore cucumber !

★

What did the chicken say when the farmer
grabbed it by the tail feathers ?

Oh, No! This is the end of me !!

★

What is a kangaroo's
favourite cowboy hero ?

Hopalong Cassidy !

★

What is a kangaroo's
favourite sporting event ?

The hop-stacle race !

How do sheep block the
entrance to their fields ?

With a five baaa gate !

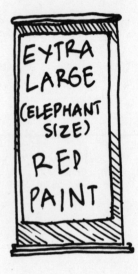

Why are elephants grey ?

**Because red paint doesn't come
in big enough tins !**

What is a vampire's favourite animal ?

The giraffe - because it has such a long neck !

Knock, knock...

Knock, Knock...
Who's there ?
Double Glazing Salesman.....hello.....hello...

Knock, knock...
Who's there ?
Mort
Mort who ?
Mort have known you would ask me that !

Knock, Knock...
Who's there ?
It's Jilly
It's Jilly who ?
It's Jilly out here - let me in !

Knock, Knock...
Who's there ?
Acton
Acton who ?
Acton stupid won't do you any good !

Knock, Knock...
Who's there ?
Eddie
Eddie who ?
Eddie minute now I'm going to sneeze !

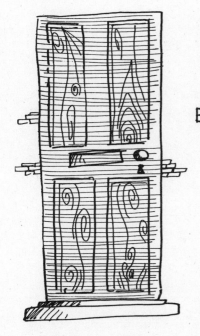

★

Knock, Knock...
Who's there ?
Barker
Barker who ?
Barker door's locked so I've come round to the front !

★

Knock, Knock...
Who's there ?
Don
Don who ?
Don worry - I'm not a burglar !

★

Knock, Knock...
Who's there ?
Carrie
Carrie who ?
Carrie this shopping in for me, it weighs a ton !

★

Knock, Knock...
Who's there ?
Fred
Fred who ?
Fred you'll have to open the door to find out !

Knock, Knock...
Who's there ?
Geoff
Geoff who ?

Geoff to ask that question every single day ?

★

Knock, Knock...
Who's there ?
Harry
Harry who ?
Harry up it's just starting to rain !

★

Knock, Knock...
Who's there ?
Iona
Iona who ?
Iona a house just like this one !

Knock, Knock...
Who's there ?
June
June who ?
June know how long I've been waiting out here ?

Knock, Knock...
Who's there ?
Ken
Ken who ?
Ken you not guess ?

★

Knock, Knock...
Who's there ?
Can you Linda
Can you Linda who ?
Can you Linda me a cup of sugar ?

★

Knock, Knock...
Who's there ?
Mary
Mary who ?
Mary Christmas !

★

Knock, Knock...
Who's there ?
Nige
Nige who ?
Nige to see you, to see you Nige !

Knock, Knock...
Who's there ?
Oscar
Oscar who ?
Oscar nother question for goodness sake !

Knock, Knock...
Who's there ?
Pete
Pete who ?
Pete after me, 'I am going to open the door now...'

★

Knock, Knock...
Who's there ?
Ronnie
Ronnie who ?
Ronnie nose - need a hanky - let me in - quick !

Knock, Knock...
Who's there ?
Stella
Stella who ?
Stella same person who was here last time you asked !

Knock, Knock...
Who's there ?
Tone
Tone who ?
Tone keep asking me that same old question !

Knock, Knock...
Who's there ?
Unger
Unger who ?
Unger the doormat is where you'll find the key !

Knock, Knock...
Who's there ?
Val
Val who ?
Val how am I supposed to know ?!

Knock, Knock...
Who's there ?
Wanda
Wanda who ?
Wanda know - open the door and find out !

Knock, Knock...
Who's there ?
Xavier
Xavier who ?
Xavier anything for the jumble sale ?

Knock, Knock...
Who's there ?
Annie
Annie who ?
Annie chance you'll open this door ?

★

Knock, Knock...
Who's there ?
Barbara
Barbara who ?
Barbara black sheep !

★

Knock, Knock...
Who's there ?
Carla
Carla who ?
**Carla doctor, your door knocker
has just fallen off and broken my toe !**

★

Knock, Knock...
Who's there ?
Deb
Deb who ?
Deb better be a good reason for keeping me waiting
out here!

Knock, Knock...
Who's there ?
Emma
Emma who ?
Emma not going to tell you again !

Knock, Knock...
Who's there ?
Fanny
Fanny who ?
Fanny how you always ask that question ?!

Knock, Knock...
Who's there ?
Arthur
Arthur who ?
Arthur gotten again !

Knock, Knock...
Who's there ?
Eileen Dover
Eileen Dover who ?
Eileen Dover your fence and broke it !

Knock, Knock...
Who's there ?
Herbert
Herbert who ?
Herbert you come to the door and see for yourself !

Knock, Knock...
Who's there ?
Morse
Morse who ?
Morse come in as quickly as possible !

Knock, Knock...
Who's there ?
Nipper
Nipper who ?
**Nipper round the back and
pass my spectacles !**

Knock, Knock...
Who's there ?
Oscar
Oscar who ?
Oscar a silly question...

Knock, Knock...
Who's there ?
Phil
Phil who ?
Phil this cup with sugar would you, I've just run out !

EMPTY

Knock, Knock...
Who's there ?
Quad
Quad who ?
Quad you want to know for ?

Knock, Knock...
Who's there ?
Russell
Russell who ?
Russell be home in a minute - put the kettle on !

Knock, Knock...
Who's there ?
Sandy
Sandy who ?
Sandy you living next door innit ?!

Knock, Knock...
Who's there ?
Tamara
Tamara who ?
Tamara's my birthday. Don't forget !

★

Knock, Knock...
Who's there ?
Urquart
Urquart who ?
Urquart just broke down, can you call the AA ?

★

Knock, Knock...
Who's there ?
Wendy
Wendy who ?
Wendy door finally
opens you can see for yourself ! !

★

Knock, Knock...
Who's there ?
Vera
Vera who ?
Vera long way from
home and need a
map !

★

Knock, Knock...
Who's there ?
Xara
Xara who ?
Xara front door the same colour as this yesterday !

Knock, Knock...
Who's there ?
Posh
Posh who ?
Posh the door open and you'll see !

Knock, Knock...
Who's there ?
Euripides
Euripides who ?
Euripides trousers you have to buy some more !

Knock, Knock...
Who's there ?
Ben
Ben who ?
Ben down the supermarket, give us
a hand with these bags !

Knock, Knock...
Who's there ?
Clara
Clara who ?
Clara space for the
shopping bags
like Ben told you to !

Knock, Knock...
Who's there ?
Lucy
Lucy who ?
Lucy Lastic !

Knock, Knock...
Who's there ?
Miguel
Miguel who ?
Miguel friends packed me in !

★

Knock, Knock...
Who's there ?
Paul
Paul who ?
Paul the other one it's got bells on !

★

Knock, Knock...
Who's there ?
John
John who ?
John know I'm getting tired standing out here !

★

Knock, Knock...
Who's there ?
Atish
Atish who ?
Bless You !

Knock, Knock...
Who's there ?
Moore
Moore who ?
Moore or less the same person as before !

Knock, Knock...
Who's there ?
Carrie
Carrie who ?
Carrie this suitcase upstairs for me...

Knock, Knock...
Who's there ?
Julienne
Julienne who ?
Julienne against that front door all day ?

Knock, Knock...
Who's there ?
Carter
Carter who ?
Carter pillar !

Knock, Knock...
Who's there ?
Toulouse
Toulouse who ?
**Toulouse are better than one in a
busy house I always say !**

★

Knock, Knock...
Knock, Knock...
Who's there ?
Carmen
Carmen who ?
**Carmen to the front room and
look through the window !**
★

Knock, Knock...
Who's there ?
Furze
Furze who ?
Furze I'm concerned you can keep the door closed !

Knock, Knock...
Who's there ?
Germaine
Germaine who ?
Germaine I can't come in unless I tell you ?

Knock, Knock...
Who's there ?
Mush
Mush who ?
Mush you always ask me this ?

Knock, Knock...
Who's there ?
Hilda
Hilda who ?
Hilda 'owt for a laugh !

Knock, Knock...
Who's there ?
Mandy
Mandy who ?
Mandy lifeboats !

Knock, Knock...
Who's there ?
Frank
Frank who ?
Frank you for asking !

Knock, Knock...
Who's there ?
Egon
Egon who ?
Egon down the shops !

Knock, Knock...
Who's there ?
Harmony
Harmony who ?
Harmony times do I have to tell you ?!

Knock, Knock...
Who's there ?
Sitter
Sitter who ?
Sitter good time to come round ?

Knock, Knock...
Who's there ?
Don
Don who ?
**Don be afraid....look into
my eyes....you are feeling sleepy...**

Knock, Knock...
Who's there ?
Ma
Ma who ?
Ma car broke down again !

Knock, Knock...
Who's there ?
A guest
A guest who ?
A guest you wouldn't recognise my voice !

★

Knock, Knock...
Who's there ?
Arnie
Arnie who ?
Arnie chance of coming in ?

★

Knock, Knock...
Who's there ?
Dan
Dan who ?
Dan Dan Dan Dan Daaaannnn !

★

Knock, Knock...
Who's there ?
Carrie
Carrie who ?
Carrie on like this
and I'll freeze to
death out here !

★

Knock, Knock...
Who's there ?
Hal
Hal who ?
Halloo !

Knock, Knock...
Who's there ?
A ghost
A ghost who ?
Thought it would scare you !

Knock, Knock...
Who's there ?
Kenya
Kenya who ?
Kenya please just open the door !?

★

Knock, Knock...
Who's there ?
France
France who ?
France y meeting you here !

★

Knock, Knock...
Who's there ?
Adolf

Adolf who ?
Adolf ball hit me in de mouf !

★

Knock, Knock...
Who's there ?
Chris
Chris who ?
Chris Packet, but my friends call me Russell !

Knock, Knock...
Who's there ?
Iona
Iona who ?
Iona have eyes for you !

★

Knock, Knock...
Who's there ?
Tinkerbell
Tinkerbell who ?
Tinkerbell would look nice on my bike !

★

Knock, Knock...
Who's there ?
Justin
Justin who ?
Just in time to open the door for me !

★

Knock, Knock...
Who's there ?
Maquis
Maquis who ?
Maquis just snapped in the lock !

Knock, Knock...
Who's there ?
Isabell
Isabell who ?
Isabell not working ?

Knock, Knock...
Who's there ?
Jethro
Jethro who ?
Jethro people out if they can't pay their bill ?

Knock, Knock...
Who's there ?
Amos
Amos who ?
Amosquito bit me !

★

Knock, Knock...
Who's there ?
Lettuce
Lettuce who ?
Lettuce in and you'll find out !

★

Knock, Knock...
Who's there ?
Ivor
Ivor who ?
**Ivor message
for a Mr Smith ?!**

★

Knock, Knock...
Who's there ?
Sid
Sid who ?
Sid down next to me !

Knock, Knock...
Who's there ?
Shirley
Shirley who ?

Shirley you know the sound of my voice by now ?

Knock, Knock...
Who's there ?
Midas
Midas who ?
Midas well open the door and find out !

Knock, Knock...
Who's there ?
Jester
Jester who ?
Jester minute I've forgotten !

Knock, Knock...
Who's there ?
Harry
Harry who ?
Harry up and let me in !

Knock, Knock...
Who's there ?
Caine
Caine who ?
Caine you see me through the glass ?

Knock, Knock...
Who's there ?
Yul
Yul who ?
Yul find out when you open the door

Knock, Knock...
Who's there ?
Cattle
Cattle who ?
Cattle get out if you open the door,
I'll come in through the window !

★

Knock, Knock...
Who's there ?
And your old lady
And your old lady who ?
I didn't know you could yodel !

★

Knock, Knock...
Who's there ?
Doris
Doris who ?
Doris closed – that's why I'm having to knock !

Knock, Knock...
Who's there ?
Europe
Europe who ?
Europe bright and early today !

Knock, Knock...
Who's there ?
Orang
Orang who ?
Orang the doorbell but it doesn't seem to work, so now I'm knocking !

Knock, Knock...
Who's there ?
Alf
Alf who ?
Alf feed the cat while you're on holiday !

Knock, Knock...
Who's there ?
Stephanie
Stephanie who ?
Stephanie me - who else could it be !

Knock, Knock...
Who's there ?
Witch doctor
Witch doctor who ?
The one with the long stripy scarf !

Knock, Knock...
Who's there ?
Wooden shoe
Wooden shoe who ?
Wooden shoe like to see ?

Knock, Knock...
Who's there ?
May-Belle
May-Belle who ?
May-Belle don't work either, so I'm knocking !

Knock, Knock...
Who's there ?
Noah
Noah who ?
Noah a good place to hide from this rain ?

Knock, Knock...
Who's there ?
Will
Will who ?
Will I ever get in !?

Knock, Knock...
Who's there ?
Luke
Luke who ?
Luke out - the Martians are landing !

Knock, Knock...
Who's there ?
Mindy
Mindy who ?
Mindy porch !

Knock, Knock...
Who's there ?
Othello
Othello who ?
Othello could freeze to death out here !

Knock, Knock...
Who's there ?
Fools Rachid
Fools Rachid who ?
Fools Rachid where angels fear to tread !

Knock, Knock...
Who's there ?
Oasis
Oasis who ?
Oasis, it's your brother, I forget me key !

Knock, Knock...
Who's there ?
Mickey
Mickey who ?
Mickey don't fit - have you changed the lock ?

Knock, Knock...
Who's there ?
Kong
Kong who ?
Kong ratulations you've won the lottery !

Knock, knock...
Who's there ?
Amanda...
Amanda who ?
Amanda last step - open the door !

Knock, knock...
Who's there ?
Dell...
Dell who ?
Dell never know I was here if you don't
tell them !

Knock, knock...
Who's there ?
Toodle...
Toodle who ?
Where are you going - I only just got here !

Knock Knock...
Who's there ?
Joanna...
Joanna who ?
Joanna stop asking stupid questions
and let me in !

Knock Knock...
Who's there ?
Ant...
Ant who ?
Ant I told you already ?

Knock Knock Knock...
Who's there ?
Moses...
Moses who ?
Moses if I knock 3 times you'll let me in !

Knock Knock...
Who's there ?
Kent...
Kent who ?
Kent you fix the doorbell ?

Knock Knock...
Who's there ?
Yul...
Yul who ?
**Yul never know if you don't
open the door will you ? !**

Knock Knock...
Who's there ?
Your maths teacher...
hello...hello....Is anyone
there...?

Knock Knock...
Who's there ?
Isabel...
Isabel who ?
Isabel a legal requirement on a bicycle ?

Knock Knock...
Who's there ?
Superman...
Superman who ?
You know I can't reveal my secret identity !

Knock Knock...
Who's there ?
Tish...
Tish who ?
Bless you !

★

Knock Knock...
Who's there ?
Twitter...
Twitter who ?
You got an owl in there ?

★

Knock Knock...
Who's there ?
Cook...
Cook who ?
**That's the first one I've
heard this year !**

★

Knock Knock...
Who's there ?
Snow...
Snow who ?
Snow joke being out here
in the cold, let me in !

Knock Knock...
Who's there ?
Nona...
Nona who ?
Nona your business !

Knock, Knock...
Who's there ?
Sinbad
Sinbad who ?
Sinbad condition your front door !

Knock Knock...
Who's there ?
Alec...
Alec who ?
Alec to see you guess !

★

Knock Knock...
Who's there ?
Les...
Les who ?
Les cut the small talk - just open the door !

Knock Knock...
Who's there ?
Wendy...
Wendy who ?
Wendy red red robin goes bob bob
bobbin along...

Knock Knock...
Who's there ?
Jim...
Jim who ?
Jim mind if I stay here tonight ?

Knock Knock...
Who's there ?
Dooby Doobid...
Dooby Doobid who ?
Ah ! A Frank Sinatra fan !

Knock Knock...
Who's there ?
Kungf...
Kungf who ?
No need to threaten me !

Knock Knock...
Who's there ?
Police...
Police who ?
Police let me in, I'm freezing out here !

Knock Knock...
Who's there ?
Marky...
Marky who ?
Markys stuck in
the keyhole, can you
open it from your side ?

★

Knock Knock...
Who's there ?
Pat...
Pat who ?
Actually it's Steve, I was just doing
an impersonation of Pat !

★

Knock Knock...
Who's there ?
The Cilla...
The Cilla who ?
The Cilla beggar
who's forgotten
her key again !

Knock Knock...
Who's there ?
Your maths teacher...
This is a recording...there's no one here
at the moment !

★

Knock Knock...
Who's there ?
Aliens...
Aliens who ?
**Just how many Aliens
do you know ?**

★

Knock Knock...
Who's there ?
Guess...
Guess who ?
**Hang on, haven't we got this mixed
up somehow ?**

★

Knock Knock...
Who's there ?
Boo...
Boo who ?
No need to get upset, it's only a game !

Knock Knock...
Who's there ?
Mike...
Mike who ?
**Mike car won't start, can I
come in and phone the RAC ?**

Knock Knock...
Who's there ?
Carol...
Carol who ?
**Carol singers – you must
have heard us we've been
at it for 20 minutes !**

Knock Knock...
Who's there ?
Phil...
Phil who ?
Phil this bag with money,
I'm a burglar !

Knock Knock...
Who's there ?
The man from next door...
The man from next door who ?
The man from next door who has clearly come home
to the wrong house, sorry !

Knock Knock...
Who's there ?
Alec...
Alec who ?
Alec your front door !

★

Knock Knock...
Who's there ?
Haydn...
Haydn who ?
Haydn like it at all !

★

Knock Knock...
Who's there ?
Ivan...
Ivan who ?
Ivan to come in - open the door !

★

Knock Knock...
Who's there ?
Josie...
Josie who ?
Josie any reason to keep me
waiting out here ?

Knock Knock...
Who's there ?
The Spice Girls...
Come in, come in, how rude of me to keep you waiting...

Knock Knock...
Who's there ?
Jeanie...
Jeanie who ?
Jeanie comprend pas - je suis Francais !

Knock Knock...
Who's there ?
Bill...
Bill who ?
Bill-ieve it or not this is a joke !

Knock Knock...
Who's there ?
Bert...
Bert who ?
Bert surely you recognise my voice !

Knock Knock...
Who's there ?
Ernie...
Ernie who ?
Ernie chance of you opening the door ?

Knock Knock...
Who's there ?
Norman...
Norman who ?
**Norman gets past this door
without your permission do they ? !**

Knock Knock...
Who's there ?
Ivor...
Ivor who ?
Ivor key of my own now !

Knock, knock...
Who's there ?
Ken...
Ken who ?
Ken I please come in now I want to play
something else ?

Knock, Knock...
Who's there ?
Avenue !
Avenue who ?
Avenue guessed yet ?

Knock Knock...
Who's there ?
Joke...
Joke who ?
Joke keep everyone waiting this long ?

Knock Knock...
Who's there ?
Bert...
Bert who ?
Bert you'll never guess !?

Who's there ?
The Witch...
The Witch who ?
Bless you !

Knock, knock...
Who's there ?
Gunga Din...
Gunga Din who ?
Gunga Din the door's locked !

Knock, knock...
Who's there ?
Nige...
Nige who ?
Nige who believe it's me ?

Knock Knock...
Go away ! I'm reading the
next section !

Knock Knock...
Who's there ?
Colin...
Colin Who ?
Colin me names is going to get
you into big trouble !

★

Knock Knock...
Who's there ?
Frank...
Frank who ?
Frankenstein !

Knock Knock...
Who's there ?
Geezer...
Geezer who ?
Geezer couple of minutes and
I'll pick this lock !

★

Knock Knock...
Who's there ?
Tim...
Tim who ?
T-I-M-B-E-R !@*!!

Knock Knock...
Who's there ?
L.E....
L.E. who ?
L.E. Funt !

Knock Knock...
Who's there ?
Kipper...
Kipper who ?
Kipper your hands off
my ice cream !

Knock Knock...
Who's there ?
Carl...
Carl who ?
Carl this a warm reception !?

Knock Knock...
Who's there ?
Oomaht...
Oomaht who ?
Have you dropped something
on your foot ?

Knock Knock...
Who's there ?
Jess...
Jess who ?
Jess open the door will you !!

Knock Knock...
Who's there ?
Snow...
Snow who ?
Snow use - I can't remember

Knock Knock...
Who's there ?
Ivor...
Ivor who ?
**Ivor got my fingers stuck
in your letter flap !**

Knock Knock...
Who's there ?
Apple...
Apple who ?
Apple the door too hard and
hit myself in the nose !

★

Knock Knock...
Who's there ?
Only Joe...
Only Joe who ?
Only Joking,
it's me really !

★

Knock Knock...
Who's there ?
Timbukt...
Timbukt who ?
That's right !
How can you
see through a
solid door !!

★

Knock Knock...
Who's there ?
Pop...
Pop who ?
Pop round and unlock the back door –
my wellies are all muddy !

★

Knock Knock...
Who's there ?
Laetitia...
Laetitia who ?
Crikey, sounds like your
cold has turned into flu !

★

Knock Knock...
Who's there ?
Wee Spencer...
Wee Spencer who ?
Wee spencer long
out here
waiting we're
freezing !

★

Knock Knock...
Who's there ?
Kurt...
Kurt who ?
Kurt out that last joke - it's terrible !

★

Knock Knock...
Who's there ?
Dennis...
Dennis who ?
Dennis must be
the right place -
he said you'd
ask that !

★

Knock Knock...
Who's there ?
Tinkerbell...
Tinkerbell who ?
Tinkerbell would save me having to
do all this knocking !

★

Knock Knock...
Who's there ?
Chester...
Chester who ?
Chester man delivering a parcel !

★

Knock Knock...
Who's there ?
A. Roland...
A. Roland who ?
**A Roland butter
would be very nice -
do you have any !**

★

Knock Knock...
Who's there ?
Ouvrez...
Ouvrez who ?
Ouvrez la porte, s'il-te-plait !
(French pen-pal over for a visit)

267

Knock Knock...
Who's there ?
Gordon...
Gordon who ?
Gordon tired of standing here I can tell you !

★

Knock Knock...
Who's there ?
Luke...
Luke who ?
**Luke through the little spyglass
and you'll see !**

★

Knock Knock...
Who's there ?
June...
June who ?
**June know how long I've been waiting
out here ?!**

Knock Knock...
Who's there ?
Creatures from another dimension...
Creatures from another dimension who ?
Creatures from another dimension
who are getting tired of waiting
to be let in, earthling !

Knock Knock...
Who's there ?
Vlad...
Vlad who ?
Vlad a long time you take
to answer the door !

Knock Knock...
Who's there ?
Ooh Ooh Ooh...
Ooh Ooh Ooh who ?
Stop playing at fire engines
and let me in !

Knock Knock...
Who's there ?
Paul...
Paul who ?
Paul the door from your side -
it seems to be stuck !

★

Knock Knock...
Who's there ?
Bart...
Bart who ?
Bart time you
opened the door !

★

Knock Knock...
Who's there ?
Daniel...
Daniel who ?
Daniel be coming round
in a bit, so leave
the door open !

Knock Knock...
Who's there ?
Wanda...
Wanda who ?
Wanda know how much
longer you're going
to keep me hanging
around out here !

★

Knock Knock...
Who's there ?
Atilla...
Atilla who ?
Atilla you open dis door I'm
a gonna stand here !

★

Knock Knock...
Who's there ?
Howill...
Howill who ?
Howill you have your
egg - fried, boiled
or scrambled ?

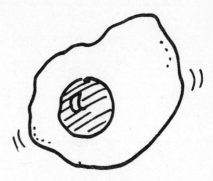

Knock Knock...
Who's there ?
Little old lady...
Little old lady who ?
Your yodelling is getting better all the time !

Knock Knock...
Who's there ?
Al...
Al who ?
Al live here - so let me in !

Knock Knock...
Who's there ?
Luke...
Luke who ?
**Luke, stop messing about
and let me in !**

Knock Knock...
Who's there ?
Fancy...
Fancy who ?
Fancy meeting you here !

Knock Knock...
Who's there ?
Phillipa...
Phillipa who ?
Phillipa hot bath - I've
just fallen in the mud !

★

Knock Knock...
Who's there ?
Dismay...
Dismay who ?
Dismay be the last time
I come round here !

★

273

Knock Knock...
Who's there ?
Ivan...
Ivan who ?
Ivan idea you already know !

Knock Knock...
Who's there ?
Mouse...
Mouse who ?
Mouse has burned down -
I'm coming to stay with you !

Knock Knock...
Who's there ?
Len...
Len who ?
Len me a key and I won't have to knock any more !

Knock Knock...
Who's there ?
Izzy...
Izzy who ?
Izzy ever going to fit a doorbell ?!

Knock Knock...
Who's there ?
Carlos...
Carlos who ?
Carlos sometime and we'll arrange
a game of football !

Knock Knock...
Who's there ?
Vera...
Vera who ?
Vera the right keys ?!

Knock Knock...
Who's there ?
Dinner...
Dinner who ?
Dinner where me key is !

Knock, Knock...
Who's there ?
Gladice...
Gladice who ?
Gladice nice weather if you're going to keep
me waiting out here all day !

★

Knock, Knock...
Who's there ?
Shirley
Shirley who ?
Shirley we don't have to go through this
rigmarole everytime I come home from work !

★

Knock Knock...
Who's there ?
Lewis...
Lewis who ?
Lewis doorknob's come
off in my hand !

★

Monster Mayhem

Mum, I've decided I don't like my
brother after all !

Well, just eat the chips and leave him
on the side of the plate !

What do monsters eat ?

Shepherds Pie
and
Ploughmans Lunch

Why are monsters always falling out
with each other ?

There's always a bone of contention !

What was the name of the monster in the 3 bears ?

Ghouldilocks !

What are a monster's favourite fairground rides?

The Helter Skeleton!

or the

Roller Ghoster!

Which monster is the most untidy?

The Loch Mess Monster

What songs do they play at ghostly discos?

Haunting melodies!

What does a young monster call his parents ?

Mummy and Deady !

What do you call a monster airline steward ?

A Fright attendant !

★

Why was the monster catching centipedes ?

He wanted scrambled legs for breakfast !

What game do ghostly mice play at parties ?

Hide and Squeak !

Why did the monster buy an axe ?

Because he wanted to get ahead in life !

Why did the monster eat his music teacher ?

His Bach was worse than his bite !

Why was the monster scared of the computer?

Because its memory had a killer bite!

What position do monsters play in football?

They are the ghoul posts!

Why do monsters have lots of nightmares?

They like to take their work
to bed with them!

What game do young monsters play ?

Corpse and Robbers !

What do monsters like to pour on their Sunday dinner ?

Grave - y !

Where do monster go on their American holidays ?

Death Valley !

How does Frankenstein's monster eat ?

He bolts his food down !

Why should you never touch a monster's tail?

**Because it is the end of the monster,
and it could also be the end of you!**

Why did the monster comedian like playing to skeletons?

Because he knew how to tickle their funny bones!

During which age did mummies live?

The Band - Age!

Eat your sprouts,
son, they'll put
colour in your
cheeks!

**But I don't want
green cheeks!**

★

What do you call a monster that comes to
your home to collect your laundry ?

An Undie-taker !

★

What is the first thing a monster does
when you give him an axe ?

Writes out a chopping list !

★

Which room in your home can ghouls not enter?

The living room!

Why did the monster have twins in his lunchbox?

In case he fancied seconds!

What job could a young monster do?

Chop assistant!

How did the monster cook the local hairdresser?

On a barbercue!

What do monsters like for breakfast?

Dreaded Wheat!

What did the metal monster have on his gravestone ?

Rust In Peace !

What do monsters have at tea time ?

Scream cakes !

What did the mummy monster say to her child at the dining table ?

Don't spook with your mouth full !

What is a young monsters favourite TV programme ?

BOO Peter !

Where do monsters live ?

Bury !

Why didn't the skeleton fight the monster ?

He didn't have the guts !

How many monsters would it take to fill
this room ?

No idea, I'd be off after the first one arrived !

What do you do if a ghoul rolls his eyes at you ?

just pick them up and roll them back !

Why was the monster hanging round
the pond with a net ?

He was collecting the ingredients for toad in the hole !

Where do skeletons keep their money ?

In a joint account !

Who was one of James Bond's spooky enemies ?

Ghouldfinger !

What has 50 legs ?

A centipede cut in half !

What sort of curry do monsters make
from their victims hearts ?

Tikka !

Why did the monster have a sprinter in his lunchbox ?

He liked fast food !

Some monster holidays...

Good Fryday !
(Good for frying anyone who gets close
enough to grab !)

Eater Sunday and Eater Monday !
(Monsters don't have eggs !)

Guy Forks Night !
(Stay at home on November
5th if you are called Guy !)

Crisps and Eve !
(Another traditional monster
recipe !)

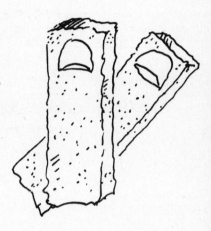

Why are monsters
so horrible ?

It's in the blood !

Why do monsters breed fish with hands ?

So they can have fish fingers with their chips !

★

What do monsters eat if the catch someone
breaking into their home ?

Beef burglers !

What do monsters make with cars ?

Traffic jam !

Why do monsters never eat police officers ?

They hate truncheon meat !

Did you hear about the monster who asked if he could leave the dining table ?

His mum said yes, she would put it in the fridge and he could eat it later !

Some foreign holiday resorts favoured by monsters...

Eat a Lee !

Belch um !

Gnaw Wayne !

Sweet Den

What do headless monsters eat ?

Chops !

What do Italian monsters eat ?

Spookgetti !

Which monster monkey thinks he can sing?

King Song!

What do you call a monster with an
axe buried in his head?

Nothing - it's perfectly normal for monsters!

Who patrols the graveyard at night?

A fright watchman!

What did the policeman say to the
monster with three heads?

Hello, hello, hello!

Why was the monster's head sticky ?

Because he styled his hair with a honey comb !

What do you have to get if you invite monsters
round to your house for a party ?

A new house !

What tune to ghosts sing their babies
to sleep with ?

Ghoulden slumbers !

Why do skeletons love Doctor McCoy
on Star Trek ?

Because he's called bones too !

What should you take if a monster
invites you for dinner ?

Someone who can't run as fast as you !

Why do vampires have to write so many letters ?

They have to reply to their fang clubs !

The Haunted House

by

Hugo First

Mummy, what is a vampire ?

**Be quiet dear and drink your blood
before it clots !**

What do you call an evil,
8 foot tall, green, hairy monster ?

Whatever he tells you to !

What is a monster's favourite handicraft ?

Tie and Die !

What do monsters do at parties ?

**They eat I scream and jelly babies
and play haunt the thimble !**

★

What's the name of that very
scary all girl band ?

You mean the Spice Ghouls !

It's no good locking your door - monsters can
always get in !

They have a set of skeleton keys !

★

Doctor, said the cannibal, I have this terrible stomach ache !

You must have eaten someone who disagreed with you !

A vampire's coffin fell off the back of a lorry and started rolling down a steep hill. The vampire knew exactly what to do. He went into a local chemist and asked if they had any sore throat sweets to stop his coffin !

Where do vampires keep their savings ?

In a blood bank !

Did you hear about the baby monster who had hundreds of little holes all over his face ?

He was learning to eat with a fork !

Where do ghosts practise frightening people ?

At swooniversity !

What do ghosts write their letters on?

Type - frighters !

How do mummies keep a secret ?

They keep it under wraps !

What do you call a monster who never
blows his nose ?

The bogeyman !

Why do skeletons rub themselves all over with towels
when they've been swimming ?

To get bone dry !

What is a sea monsters favourite takeaway?

Fish and ships with worry sauce !

★

Menu

Shepherd Pie

or

Ploughman Lunch

followed by

Necktarines with double scream

What sort of horses do monsters ride?

Night mares!

★

When a monster's hungry and needs to be fed,
it's no good hiding under the bed!
He'll roll you in the mattress,
till you're buried like a mole,
then chomp you down in two big bites,
like a giant sausage roll!

★

What did the monster say when it saw someone going past on a mountain bike ?

Ah ! Meals on wheels !

What is a vampire's favourite soup ?

Scream of mushroom !

Monster - Waiter, this is ordinary spaghetti - I ordered worms !

Waiter - Ah, I wondered why the man on the table next to you was being sick in the toilet !

Sally - What is the difference between a monster and a digestive biscuit ?

Jim - I don't know.

Sally - Have you ever tried dunking a monster in your tea?

A ghost went into a pub at midnight and asked the barman for a whisky. "Sorry sir," replied the barman, "we aren't allowed to serve spirits after closing time."

★

Party games for monsters...

Pass the person
and
Swallow the leader !

★

What sort of monsters have wavy hair ?

Sea monsters !

★

Which railway company employs ghosts ?

British Wail !
(They work as in-spectres)

What do Hungarian ghosts eat ?

Ghoulash !

What position do ghosts play in football teams ?

Ghoulkeepers !

What do you call a relaxed ghost ?

Ghoul as a cucumber !

What do you call a haunted set square ?

A trian-ghoul !

Where do ghouls go for their holidays
and how do they get there ?

**They fly British Scareways to
the Isle of Fright !**

Why do travelling salesmen always try to
sell things to vampires ?

Because they know they are suckers !

Where was Frankenstein's head made ?

Bolton !

What is the first thing a vampire sinks his fangs into after the dentist has sharpened and polished them?

The dentist's neck!

What do ghostly boy scouts sing round the camp fire?

Ging - gang - ghouly - ghouly - ghouly - ghouly - gotcha!

Why are ghosts no good at telling lies?

Because you can always see through them!

Where do monsters live?

Crawley!

What sort of vampires prey on elephants ?

The very stupid ones !

What do ghosts do in the countryside ?

They go fox haunting !

What do you do to keep ghosts fit ?

Call in an exercisist !

*A new ghost was sitting in bed reading
when an old ghost walked through the wall
and into his room.*
"It's no good," said the new ghost, "I still don't
understand how you do it"
**"Watch," said the old ghost, "and I'll go through it
again !"**

What is a monster's favourite game ?

Hide and Shriek !

Why aren't robots afraid of monsters ?

Because they have nerves of steel !

Did you hear about the witch who was caught
speeding on her broomstick ?

She had a brush with the law !

What is a monster's favourite shape ?

A vicious circle !

Where do monsters send their dirty washing ?

The dry screamers !

and they send it in a hauntry basket !

What is a vampire's favourite convenience food ?

Black pudding !

What do baby monsters sometimes suffer from ?

Chicken spooks !

★

What do monsters read in the
newspaper every morning ?

Their horror - scope !

What do you call a monster with
a wooden leg ?

Long John Slither !

★

Why do vampire families never fight ?

Because they can't stand bad blood !

Where do ghosts read the news ?

In a whhhooooosspaper !

What sort of music do mummies like best ?

Wrap music !

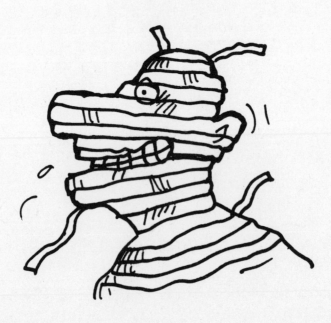

What do you call a vampire who spends all
his time in the pub ?

Count Drunkula !

What is a sea monsters favourite toy ?

A sea-saw !

Gnomes have dreadful table manners...

...they are always Goblin their food !

What do ghosts leave their children when they die ?

All their unwordly goods !

Why do vampires take their football so seriously ?

Because there is always so much at stake !

Menu
Sean cocktail
or
Dawn on the cob
followed by
I scream !
(and so would you if you had been there !)

A werewolf can't die
a vampire can fly
a monster can bite off your head.
It's no wonder I'm scared'
cos the noise I just heard...

means they're all hiding under my bed !

What TV proramme do monsters watch ?

Glad He Ate Us !

What is a monster's favourite soup ?

Any flavour, as long as it's a hearty meal !

What is the best way to let a vampire know he's not welcome at your party ?

Offer him a garlic sausage sandwich in a hot cross bun, and tell him there is stake to follow !

★

What did the vampire say when it saw the queue at the doctor's surgery ?

Necks please !

★

Monster - What is that smoke coming from the kitchen ?

Waiter -Well, you asked us to fry you a vicar - that's holy smoke !

★

315

Sally - Did you make a sandwich with half
a monster in it ?

Jim - certainly not !

Sally - Oh! Then you must have
eaten half already !

★

How can you
help a starving
monster ?

Give him a hand !

★

What can you buy a monster to decorate
his Christmas tree ?

Furry lights !

★

Why do monsters let out a
blood curdling scream?

**Because otherwise it would be too runny
to spread on their sandwiches!**

Which shop employs ghosts?

Marks & Spectres

What magazine do houseproud
monsters read?

Ghouled Housekeeping!

What do monster football fans sing?

Ghoul never walk alone!

Why does Cinderella play football so badly?

**Well, so would you if you had
a pumpkin for a coach!**

How can you tell if a monster is friendly?

**Give him a sandwich and see if he
bites the hand that feeds him!**

What is the essential feature on a
witch's computer?

The Spell-checker!

What do monsters take
to a house warming party?

Matches !

★

Monster - How much are those kittens
in the window?

Pet shop owner - Twelve pounds apiece.

**Monster - Right. I'll have a piece of the black one and
a piece of the tabby !**

What did the stupid monster buy
when the joke shop ran out
of itching powder ?

A scratch card !

★

What football team do vampires support ?

Fangchester United !

★

What did the witch say to her cat?

You look familiar!

Why does Dracula like old fashioned things?

He's never liked anything new fangled!

What sound do baby ghosts make when they cry?

Boo Hoo!
or
they wail!

A monster went to his doctor
with acid indigestion...

"It's no good", said his doctor, "you will just
have to stop drinking acid !"

Why does Dracula wear bright red braces ?

To hold his trousers up !

What is Dracula's favourite TV game show ?

Count Down !

What did the doctor say to the ghost ?

Sorry, but I can't see you at the moment !

Why do cricketers carry garlic
when they are on tour ?

To keep away vampire bats !

Name another of James Bond's spooky enemies ?

Doctor Nnnnnnnooooooooooo !

I know a vampire who spends all morning
writing letters...

Well, he has to reply to his fang mail !

Did you hear about the vampire
builder who starved to death ?

He couldn't get blood out of a stone !

★

What sort of pets do monsters keep ?

Ghould - fish !

★

What is that ghost doing in the January sales?

Bargain haunting!

What do you do to keep ghosts fit?

Run faster!

In the old days ghosts had to take exams before they were allowed to go haunting. They had to have Ooohhh levels!

What was the ghost put in jail for?

Driving without due scare and attention!

A monster arrived at his friend's house with a skeleton in a bag...

....he said "I've got a bone to pick with you!"

I'd tell you the story of the vampire's broken tooth...

...but there's no point !

★

What do you do with a blue monster ?

Try and cheer him up a bit !

Why did Frankenstein's monster like
stand up comedians ?

Because they kept him in stitches !

What do you think when you see a monster ?

'I hope he hasn't seen me !'

Which Shakespeare play is about
vampires in Scotland ?

Drac-beth !

What sort of monster wakes you up in the morning with a nice cup of tea ?

A mummy !

Why are ghosts so bad at telling lies ?

Because you can always see through them !

Why do skeletons not trust archaeologists ?

Because they indulge in skullduggery !

Barmy Brain Teasers

What did the bull say when he came back
from the china shop?

I've had a really smashing time!

What's the special offer at the pet shop
this week ?

Buy one cat - get one flea !

When do 2 and 2 make more than 4 ?

When they make 22 !

Why were the naughty eggs sent out of the class ?

For playing practical yolks !

Why should you never listen too closely to the match?

Because you might burn your ears!

Why did the bakers work late?

Because they kneaded the dough!

What do mice sing at birthday parties?

For cheese a jolly good fellow!

How does Father Christmas start a joke?

This one will sleigh you...!

What jewelry do ghosts wear?

Tombstones!

What do mummies use to wash up?

Pharaoh liquid!

How can you sleep like a log ?

Put your bed in the fireplace !

What do space monster sweet shops sell ?

Mars bars, galaxy and milky way !

★

What can you catch and hold but never touch ?

Your breath !

★

What do you call the finest Indian wine?

Vin - daloo!

★

What are dog biscuits made from?

Collie - flour!

★

What flower do you have to keep a look out for in the garden?

Anenome!

★

Where would you find secret soup?

At the minestrone of defence!

★

What animal uses a nucracker ?

A squirrel with no teeth !

★

Why are you burying my car ?

Because you said the battery was dead !

★

Why did the man jump up and down
after taking his medicine ?

Because he forgot to shake the bottle
before he took it !

★

Which famous artist had a bad cold?

Vincent van cough!

Why did the
burglar buy a surf
board?

He wanted to start
a crime wave!

What does a toad
sit on?

A toadstool!

What does a toad
use for making
furniture?

A toad's tool!

Why don't pigs telephone one another?

Because there is too much crackling on the line!

Why are pigs no good at do-it-yourself?

Because they are ham-fisted!

★

Why did the burglar break into the music shop?

He was after the lute!

Why did the burglar break into the bakers?

He wanted to steal the dough!

Why did the burglar go to the bank?

To recycle his bottles!

How do you keep a fool in suspense?

I'll tell you tomorrow!

How do you make a fool laugh on Saturday?

Tell him a joke on Wednesday!

Why must you never make a noise in a hospital?

Because you don't want to wake the sleeping pills!

What is a squirrel's favourite chocolate?

Whole nut!

Where would you find a bee ?

At the start of the alphabet !

Where is there always a queue ?

In between P and R !

What does it mean if your nose starts to run ?

It's trying to catch a cold !

Why is the Leopard the only animal that can't
hide from hunters ?

Because it is always spotted !

Why did the elephant refuse to play cards
with his two friends ?

**Because one of them was lion and
the other was a cheetah !**

How do you make a Venetian blind ?

Paint his spectacles black when he's asleep !

Who is a caveman's favourite band ?

The stones !

★

Why does a giraffe have such a long neck ?

Have you ever smelled a giraffe's feet !

Mary had a little fox,
it ate her little goat,
now everywhere that Mary goes,
she wears her fox-skin coat !

What jungle animal would you find at the North Pole ?

A lost one !

What sort of frog is covered in dots and dashes ?

A morse toad !

Where do cows go for history lessons ?

To a mooseum !

★

What does a polar bear use to keep his head warm ?

A polar ice cap !

★

What does a hard of hearing apple have in his ear ?

A lemonade !

★

How do plumbers get to work ?

By tube !

★

What sort of music do police officers like ?

Anything with a regular beat !

What do you need to electrocute
an orchestra ?

A good conductor !

Good morning Mr Butcher, do you have pig's feet ?

Certainly, sir !

Well, wear larger shoes and no-one will notice !

How do teddies like to ride horses ?

Bear back !

What do teddies take when they are
going on holiday ?

Just the bear essentials !

Who always puts thyme in his soup ?

A clockmender !

Waiter, there's a small worm in my salad !

Oh, dear, I'll tell the chef to send you a large one !

What do you give a dog for breakfast ?

Pooched eggs !

★

Why couldn't the orange call the apple on the telephone ?

Because the lime was engaged !

Why are those clothes running out of the sports shop ?

They're jogging suits !

Why do video machines always win their football matches ?

Because they have fast forwards !

Why do cows lie down together when it rains?

To keep each udder dry!

What sort of fruit would you find in a diary?

Dates!

What do vegetarians take home for wages?

A Celery!

Atissshhhooo, I don't feel very well!

Wow, I didn't know that having a cold affected your sense of touch!

Did you hear about the punk rocker who fell over and 50 others fell over at the same time?

He started a chain reaction!

What do you call a man who never pays his bills?

Owen!

Why did the doll blush ?

Because she saw the teddy bare !

When should you put your electric guitar in the fridge ?

When you want to play some really cool music !

Where is the greenest city in Europe ?

Brussels !

Which Italian city is good for wandering round ?

Rome !

Which English city has the best stock of
electrical connectors ?

Leeds !

Which French city has the best stock of paper ?

Rheims !

Why are bearded men fearless ?

Because they can never have a close shave !

★

What song do sweets sing at parties ?

For he's a jelly good fellow !

How do you write a essay on a giraffe ?

With a long ladder !

How do you shock people at a tea party ?

Serve current buns !

What says 'now you see me, now you don't...'

A nun on a zebra crossing !

Why do vampires like crossword puzzles ?

They like the crypt - ic clues !

My cellar is full of toadstools !

How do you know they're toadstools ?

There's not mushroom in there for anything else !

Why do some anglers suck their maggots?

So they can wait for a fish to bite with baited breath!

Should I give the dog some of my pie?

Certainly not, he didn't want it when I gave it to him earlier!

What shampoo do spooks use?

Wash - n - ghost!

What sort of ghosts haunt hospitals?

Surgical spirits!

How do you tell a ghost how lovely they are ?

'you're bootiful !'

★

What do you get if you cross a skunk with an owl ?

Something that stinks, but doesn't give a hoot !

★

What did the doctor give Cleopatra for her headache ?

An asp - irin !

What do you give a ghost with a headache ?

AAAAGGGGHHHHspirin !

Where do vampires go on holiday ?

Veinice !

How do you know if a bicycle is haunted ?

Look for spooks in the wheels !

What do you call a doctor with a bright
green stethoscope ?

Doctor !

What sort of parties do vampires like best ?

Fang - cy dress parties !

Why should you never tell your secrets to a piglet ?

Because they might squeal !

★

How do rabbits go on holiday ?

By British hareways !

★

How do you talk to a hen ?

By using fowl language !

★

Who is the patron saint of toys ?

Saint Francis of a see-saw !

Which teacher won't allow sick notes ?

The music teacher !

What is a *juggernaut* ?

An empty jug !

What does B.C. stand for ?

Before calculators !

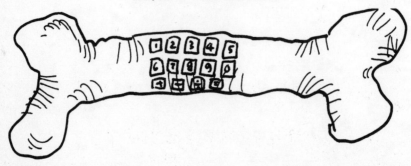

What did the stupid fencing team take to the olympics ?

5000 litres of creosote !

Which trees grow at the seaside ?

Beach trees !

How do you make a Mexican chilli ?

Take him to Iceland !

What do cannibals do at a wedding ?

They toast the bride and groom !

What is a mistake ?

An unmarried female bank robber !

Why is the bookshop the tallest
building in the town ?

**Because it has the
most stories !**

Who do you ask to see if you find
a twig in your salad ?

The branch manager !

What sort of person gets paid to make faces all day ?

A clockmaker !

What happened when the vampire went insane ?

He went batty !

★

What sort of tree grows near a volcano ?

A lava tree !

What did the skunk say when the wind changed direction ?

It's all coming back to me now !

Where do you find monster snails ?

On the end of monsters' fingers !

Why must you always have holes in your socks ?

**You wouldn't be able to get your feet
in them if you didn't !**

In which battle was Alexander the Great killed ?

His last one !

What is yellow, wears glasses and sings ?

'Nana Mouskouri !

In which film does fruit rule the world ?

Planet of the grapes !

Where do squirrels keep their nuts ?

In a pan-tree !

Which is the strongest day of the week ?

Sunday - all the others are weak days !

What do you call someone who can't
stop stealing carpets ?

A rug addict !

What do you get if you
leave your
teaspoon in the cup ?

**A sharp pain in the eye
when you drink !**

Which of these is correct -
'egg yolk is white'
'egg yolk are white'

Neither - egg yolk is yellow !

Where would you find a rubber trumpet ?

In an elastic band !

What goes up but never comes down ?

Your age !

Which birds fly in formation ?

The Red Sparrows !

★

What do you call a lion with no eyes ?

Lon !

★

Why are cars rubbish at football ?

They only have one boot each !

Why did the satsuma go to the doctor ?

It wasn't peeling too good !

What music does King Neptune like ?

Sole !

Why does it snow in the Winter ?

Because it's too hot in the *Summer* !

★

What do you call a very old Dracula ?

Gran pire !

★

What do you throw for a stick insect to fetch ?

A dog !

★

What sort of fish would you find in a bird cage ?

A perch !

★

What is a vampires favourite coffee ?

Decoffinated !

★

Where do insects go to dance ?

A cricket ball !

Why is it impossible to open a locked piano lid ?

Because all the keys are on the inside !

What do you get if you read the Monster Kids' Joke Book to an Oxo cube ?

A laughing stock !

Which robot was stuck in road works ?

R 2 Detour !

★

What runs all the way round your house
without moving ?

The fence !

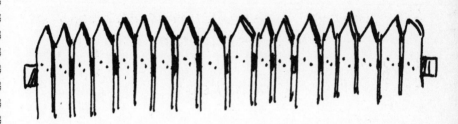

★

What show do undertakers look forward to every
year ?

The hearse of the year show !

★

How do you measure the size of fruit ?

With a green gauge !

★

What has no legs, but runs across
the bathroom floor ?

Water !

Why was the blacksmith arrested ?

For forging !

What is it called when a fish tells lies in a courtroom ?

Perchery !

Why is a bad bank like a lazy schoolboy ?

They both lose interest quickly !

What should you take if you feel run down ?

The number of the car that hit you !

How do hens dance ?

Chick to chick !

Did you hear about the Martian who went
to a plastic surgeon for a face lift ?

She wanted her face to look like a million
dollars, so the surgeon made it all
green and crinkly !

Where do Martians live ?

In greenhouses !

What do you give the man who has everything ?

Nothing !

★

Where would
you keep
sheep covered
in ink ?

In a pen !

What do you call a story that someone
tells you at breakfast every day ?

A cereal !

★

What do you call a story that someone tells you
in the car on the way to school every day ?

A mini-serial !

★

Who drives her children to school in a small car ?

A minimum !

What do vampires do before driving a car ?

They check the wing mirrors !

Why do vampires never marry ?

They are bat - chelors !

Why do woodworm have no friends ?

Because they are boring creatures !

Where can you go for a quick break by the beach ?

A seaside karate club !

How do you stop your nose from running ?

Take away its trainers !

What is the best thing to put in a sandwich ?

Your teeth !

Who writes joke books in never never land !

Peter Pun !

What do you get if you cut a comedian in two?

A half wit!

What do you get if you cross a bee with an ape?

Sting Kong!

How do jockeys send messages to each other?

With horse code!

★

What do dogs go to the hairdresser for?

A shampoodle and setter!

Why did the cow look into the crystal ball ?

To see if there was a message from the udder side !

★

What did the doctor give the deaf fisherman ?

A herring aid !

★

Who thought up the
series 'Star Trek' ?

Some bright Spock !

★

Why couldn't the astronauts land on the moon?

Because it was full!

What time is it when astronauts are hungry?

Launch time!

How can you cook turkey that really tickles the taste buds?

Leave the feathers on!

What do you call a bike that bites your bottom
when you try to get on it ?

A vicious cycle !

Why do demons and ghouls get on so
well together ?

Because demons are a ghouls best friend !

Why are lots of famous artists French ?

Because they were born in France !

Why are dentists so miserable ?

**Because they are always looking down
in the mouth !**

What did the space monster say after it had eaten a planet ?

"A Mars a day helps you work, rest and play !"

What is the name of the detective who solves all his crimes by pure accident ?

Sheer - Luck Holmes !

What is the one thing you can catch with your hands tied ?

A cold !

How do you know when your dustbin is full of toadstools ?

Because there's not mushroom inside !

What do you get if you cross a cow with a monster?

A horrible mootation!

What do you get if you drop a
piano down a coal mine?

A flat minor!

What time is it when a Chinese man
visits the dentist?

Tooth hurty!

Which is the strongest thing in the garden?

The muscle sprout!

And which is the weakest?

The weeds!

Why couldn't the squirrel finish his Meccano
model of the Forth Bridge ?

Because he'd eaten all the nuts !

Where did the colonel keep his armies ?

Up his sleevies !

Where would you find a rubber trumpet ?

In an elastic band !

Where does tea
come from ?

**In between the letters
S and U !**

What starts at the bottom
and goes all the way down
to the floor ?

Your leg !

What sits in a pram and wobbles ?

A jelly baby !

How do you make Scotch eggs ?

Feed your chickens whisky !

★

What gets bigger the more you take out of it ?

A hole !

★

How do you make a Swiss roll ?

Push him down an alp !

★

What sort of music was invented by cave men ?

Rock music !

What happened to the man who stole
a lorry load of prunes ?

He was on the run for months !

Waiter, there's a fly in my soup !

**Thank you for telling me, sir. I'd forgotten to
put that on the bill !**

How do you get rid of a boomerang ?

Throw it down a one-way street !

How does the snow queen travel about ?

By icicle !

How do you get down from a giraffe ?

You don't get down from a giraffe - you get down from a duck !

Why do cows moo ?

Because their horns don't work !

★

What is Dracula's
favourite
TV game show ?

**The Crypt-on
factor !**

What's black and white and
red all over ?

A newspaper !

What kind of nuts do the
Russians and Americans
send into space ?

Astronuts !

What sort of music do
miners like to listen to ?

Rock and coal !

*Mary had a little lamb,
it's fleece was black as soot,
and everywhere that Mary went,
its sooty foot it put !*

What do they call the back entrance to a cafeteria?

The bacteria!

★

What do you call
the room where
Eskimos train their
dogs?

The mushroom!

★

Who swings from
cake to cake?

Tarzipan!

★

Why do potatoes always know what you've done?

Because they have eyes!

★

How do you know when it's been raining
cats and dogs ?

There are lots of little poodles on the pavement !

**What do you
call a cat with
8 legs ?**

An octopus !

What do Eskimos eat for breakfast ?

Ice Crispies !

Where would you find a dog with 4 broken legs ?

Wherever you left it !

How do carpenters go on holiday ?

They fly there by plane !

Jim - Most Egyptian kings were buried with a namafor !

Joe - What's a namafor ?

Jim - Knocking nails in !

What do you call someone who puts bulls' to sleep ?

A bulldozer !

★

What happened to the cat that swallowed
some knitting ?

It had mittens !

★

What is the most useful cat
if you're looking
for something ?

A Catalogue !

★

What do you call a cat that knows how to
phone for an ambulance ?

A first aid kit !

★

WING...
WING

Why is using a telephone
so difficult
in China ?

Because there are so
many Wings and so many
Wongs, you might wing
the wong number !

Why did the man order alphabet soup ?

He wanted to eat his words !

★

Who invented the steam engine ?

No he didn't, it was Watt !

A caveman chasing dinosaurs
wants to make a bronto burger
hungry T Rex joins in too...
...hope he enjoyed his human stew !

What's the difference between a butcher and a night watchman ?

One weighs a steak, the other stays awake !

★

How do you stop an elephant stampede ?

Telephone the operator and ask to make a reverse charge call !

★

How many days of the week begin with T ?

All except Sunday, when I have coffee !

★

Where does Dracula stay when he's on holiday in America ?

The Vampire State Building !

★

What's the best thing to
put into a pie ?

Your knife and fork !

★

Why are teddies good at being spies ?

Because they can tell bear faced lies !

★

Why did the orchestra have such
bad manners ?

**They didn't know how to
conduct themselves !**

★

Where did Noah
keep all the elderly
bees ?

In his Ark-hives !

★

Good morning Mr Butcher,
do you have a sheep's
head ?

No - it's just the way I
part my hair !

★

What do you call someone who is always
working overtime ?

A clock mender !

★

Good morning sir, can I
interest you
in a pocket
calculator ?

No, thanks, I already
know how many
pockets
I've got !

Waiter, there's a fly in my soup !

Don't worry, I'll give you a reduction for the
soup he eats !

Why do mum and dad kangaroos hate rainy days ?

Because the children have to play indoors
when it rains !

Why do elephants wear green jackets ?

So they can walk across a pool table
without being seen !

What's purple and plugs into your TV set ?

An electric plum !

What is yellow and costs a million pounds ?

A banana - I lied about it costing a million pounds !

Why do vampires use
more toothpaste than
ordinary people ?

They have bat breath !

What happens when a frog
breaks down ?

He gets toad away !

What is green and goes round and round ?

An alien in a washing machine !

Where was the American declaration of
Independence signed ?

At the bottom !

PLEASE SIGN HERE ...

Why do bees buzz?

Because they don't know how to whistle!

★

Why did the stupid robber carry two bricks?

Because the jewellers shop had double glazing!

★

My friend is so thin that when we go to the park the ducks throw bread at him!

★

Why did the jogger need so many hankies?

Because his nose was always running!

★

Why was the football
pitch soggy ?

Because the
players were
always dribbling !

What do you give to
injured fruit ?

Lemonaid !

What is all that rubbish in the restaurant ?

Oh, someone left a tip !

What do chiropodists eat for breakfast ?

Corn flakes !

★

What is the difference between a March hare and a six pound note ?

One is a mad bunny, the other's bad money !

The police are looking for a burglar with a wooden leg called Blenkinsop...

...What's his other leg called ?

Jane - My boyfriend reminds me of the sea !

Joe - You mean he's strong, exciting and full of surprises ?

Jane - No, he makes me sick !

Crazy Crosses

What do you get if you cross a
fish and a deaf person?

A herring aid!

What do you get if you cross a road
with a blindfold ?

Knocked down !

What do you get if you cross a mouse
with a tin opener ?

**Something that can get the cheese from the fridge
without even opening the door !**

What do you get if you cross a car with the millennium ?

A Rover 2000 !

What do you get if you cross a
bridge with your feet ?

To the other side !

What do you get if you cross a parrot
and a scary film ?

A bad attack of the polly-wobbles !

What do you get if you cross a car
with a row of mountains ?

A Range Rover !

What do you get if you cross a wizard
and an aeroplane ?

A flying sorcerer !

What do you get if you cross a
plant pot and an infant ?

A growing child !

What do you get if you cross a
football team and a pig?

Queens Pork Rangers!

What do you get if you cross a hive of bees with a
jumper knitting pattern?

Nice and swarm!

What do you get if you...
pinch part of an elderly Scotsman's fish supper?

A chip off the old Jock!

What do you get if you cross two vicars
and a telephone line ?

A parson to parson call !

What do you get if you cross a
computer with a beefburger ?

A big mac !

What do you get if you cross a
rhinocerous with a cat ?

Very worried mice !

What do you get if you cross a sheep
with a plant ?

Cotton wool !

What do you get if you cross a sheep
with a steel bar ?

Wire wool !

★

What do you get if you cross a sheep
with an octopus ?

Jumpers with eight arms !

★

What do you get if you cross a sheep
with an outboard motor !

Baa Baa Baa Baa Baa Baa Baa Baa Baa Baa Baa Baa..

What do you get if you cross a dog
with a vegetable ?

A Jack Brussel terrier !

What do you get if you cross a sheep with a pub ?

A cocktail Baaa !

What do you get if you cross a
comedy author with a ghost ?

A crypt writer !

What do you get if you cross two
skeletons and an argument ?

A bone of contention !

This is a bone of contention !
No it isn't !
Yes it is !

What do you get if you cross a witch and a
bowl of breakfast cereal ?

Snap, cackle and pop !

What do you get if you
cross a coat and a fire ?

A blazer !

What do you get if you cross a spinach eater,
a suitmaker and a hippy ?

Popeye the tailor, man !

What do you get if you cross a shark
and Father Christmas ?

Santa jaws !

What do you get if you cross a waiter
and a slippery floor ?

Flying saucers !

What do you get if you cross a tropical
fruit and a sad dog ?

A melon collie !

What do you get if you cross a
baby and a snake ?

A rattler !

What do you get if you cross
a chicken with a kangaroo ?

Pouched eggs !

What do you get if you cross a Star Wars
robot with a sheep ?

R 2 D ewe !

What do you get if you cross a penguin
with a hungry schoolchild ?

An empty wrapper !

★

What do you get if you cross a donkey with a mole ?

Mule hills in your garden !

What do you get if you cross a chicken
with a cement lorry ?

A bricklayer !

What do you get if you cross a monster and
a bowl of breakfast cereal ?

Dreaded wheat !

What do you get if you cross a bad golfer and an
outboard motor ?

Putt putt putt putt putt putt putt putt putt...

What do you get if you cross a track suit
and a tortoise ?

A shell suit !

What do you get if you cross a cat with a cushion ?

A cat a pillow !

What do you get if you cross a skeleton
and a supermodel ?

Not an ounce of fat !

What do you get if you cross a Prime Minister
and a pair of grimy spectacles ?

Blaired vision !

What do you get if you cross a Prime Minister and a bunny ?

Blair Rabbit !

What do you get if you cross a great invention with a herb ?

A thyme machine !

What do you get if you cross a parking space and a camel ?

A camelot!

What do you get if you cross a half
open door and a queue of cars ?

Ajar of jam !

What do you get if you cross an
alien with a pair of gloves ?

Green fingers !

What do you get if you cross a sore throat
and some Christmas decorations ?

Tinselitis !

What do you get if you cross a turkey
with an octopus ?

A leg for everyone at Christmas dinner !

What do you get if you cross China
with a car horn ?

Hong King !

What do you get if you cross a bed with
a set of cricket wickets ?

A three poster !

What do you get if you cross a hat
with a mountain top ?

A peaked cap !

What do you get if you cross a
vegetable with a 26 mile run?

A Marrow - thon!

What do you get if you cross a rodent and
someone who cleans your home?

A mousekeeper!

What do you get if you cross a ghost
and a Christmas play?

A Phantomime!

What do you get if you cross a cow with a pillar box ?

Postman cow pat !

What do you get if you cross a joke book
with an Oxo cube ?

A laughing stock !

What do you get if you cross a television
personality and a jungle animal ?

A Gnus reader !

What do you get if you cross a stick insect
and a TV presenter ?

Stickolas Parsons !

What do you get if you cross a golf club
and a burrowing animal ?

A mole in one !

What do you get if you cross a surgeon
and an octopus ?

A doctorpus !

What do you get if you cross a robot
with a drinks machine ?

C - tea - P - O !

What do you get if you cross a playing card
with a fizzy drink ?

Joker cola !

What do you get if you cross a robot with a foot ?

C - 3 - P - toe !

What do you get if you drop an iron
on someone's head ?

Hard water !

What do you get if you cross a
day of the week with bubble gum?

Chewsday!

What do you get if you cross vampires
with some cheddar?

Bancheese!

What do you get if you cross an
octopus with a fountain pen?

A squidgy pen with 8 nibs that
makes all its own ink!

What do you get if you cross a horse with a
cake and a long rubber strip?

A bun - gee - gee jumper!

What do you get if you cross a toad
with a science fiction film ?

Star warts !

★

What do you get if you cross a centipede
with a children's toy ?

**A lego, lego, lego, lego, lego, lego,..............
lego, lego, lego, set**

What do you get if you cross a laundry basket
with a shopping basket ?

Man eating underpants !

What do you get if you cross a fairy and a turkey ?

A very strange Goblin !

What do you get if you cross a joke book
and two dozen eggs ?

A book with at least 24 yolks in it !

What do you get if you cross a fish
with a modelmaker ?

A scale model !

What do you get if you cross milk, fruit
and a scary film ?

A strawberry milk shake !

What do you get if you cross a pig
and a very old radio ?

Lots of crackling !

What do you get if you cross a
cricket ball and an alien ?

A bowling green !

What do you get if you cross a mountain
with hiccups ?

A volcano !

What athlete do you get if you cross
a snake and a sheep ?

A long jumper !

What do you get if you cross an ant and a calculator ?

An account - ant !

What do you get if you cross an army
and some babies ?

The infantry !

★

What do you get if
you cross a tall
building and a home
for pigs ?

A sty - scraper !

What do you get if you cross a breadcake
and a cattle rustler ?

A beef burglar !

What do you get if you cross a window
and a shirt collar ?

A pane in the neck !

What do you get if you cross a
can of oil and a mouse ?

I don't know, but at least it doesn't sqeak !

What do you get if you cross a sheep
with a discount store ?

Lots of baaaaagains !

What do you get if you cross a camel and a ghost ?

Something that goes hump in the night !

★

What do you get if
you cross a
holidaymaker
and an elephant ?

**Something that
carries its own
trunk !**

★

What do you get if
you cross a ghost
and a pair
of glasses ?

Spook - tacles !

★

What do you get if you cross a...
field of cows and a motor boat ?

Pat pat pat pat pat pat pat pat pat.....

What do you get if you cross a feather
with a carnation ?

Tickled pink !

What do you get if you cross a spider
with a football ground ?

Webley stadium !

What do you get if you cross a boy band and some
bottles of lemonade ?

A pop group !

What do you get if you cross a chimpanzee
with an oven?

A hairy griller!

What do you get if you cross a toad with someone
who tells strange jokes?

Someone with a wart sense of humour!

What do you get if you cross a
jewellers shop with a boxer?

A window full of boxing rings!

What do you get if you cross a crying baby
and a football fan ?

A footbawler !

★

What do you get if you cross an oil well
with bad manners ?

Crude oil !

★

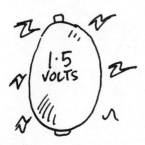

What do you get if you cross
electricity
and a chicken ?

Battery eggs !

What do you get if you cross a fish and a birdcage ?

Perch !

What do you get if you
cross a butcher and a
dance ?

A meatball !

What do you get if you
cross a scratch
on your arm and a fruit ?

A lemon sore - bit !

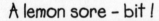

What do you get if you cross a skunk
and a winning lottery ticket ?

Stinking rich !

What do you get if you cross a ball
and a blunt instrument ?

A football club !

What do you get if you cross the sea
and a pot of chilli ?

A Mexican wave !

What do you get if you cross a donkey and a three
legged milking stool ?

A wonkey !

What do you get if you cross a sheep
and an ink cartridge ?

Something that only a sheepdog can get into a pen !

What do you get if you cross a lawn and a mattress ?

A flower bed !

What do you get if you cross a...
cat with a set of water colours ?

Pusster Paints !

What do you get if you cross a...
dog and an elephant ?

No more post !

What do you get if you cross a...
giraffe and a dog ?

Something that bites the tyres of low flying aircraft !

What do you get if you cross a...
range of mountains with a dancer ?

Something huge dancing peak to peak !

What do you get if you cross a...
penguin with a paratrooper ?

A chocolate soldier !

What do you get if you cross a...
cartoon with some bubble gum ?

A carica - chewer !

What do you get if you cross a...
fox and a policeman ?

A brush with the law !

What do you get if you cross a...
pencil with window covers ?

Blinds that draw themselves !

★

What do you get if you cross a...
postman, his pet cat and a field of cows ?

Postman pat and his black and white cow pat !

What do you get if you cross a...
pig and a flea ?

Pork scratchings !

What do you get if you cross a...
Welshman and a saint ?

Good Evans !

What do you get if you cross a...
bottle of pop and a frog ?

Croaka Cola !

What do you get if you cross a...
budgie and a clown ?

Cheep and cheerful !

What do you get if you cross a...
comedian, an owl and a tube of adhesive ?

A Wit Who Glues !

What do you get if you cross a kangaroo with a sheep?

A woolly jumper !

G'DAY!

★

What do you get if you cross a kangaroo with a line of people waiting for a bus ?

A queue jumper !

★

What do you get if you cross a policeman with a landscape artist ?

A constable !

★

What do you get if you cross an
elephant with a mouse ?

Ten foot holes in your skirting board !

What do you get
if you cross
a bear with a
cow pat ?

Winnie the Pooh !

What do you get if you cross a chicken with a skunk ?

A fowl smell !

What do you get if you cross a fly
with a detective ?

A police insector !

What do you get if you cross a pig
with an ambulance ?

A Hambulance !

What do you get if you cross
a window cleaner with a giraffe ?

A window cleaner who doesn't need any ladders !

What do you get if
you cross a pig
with Dracula ?

A Hampire !

What do you get if you cross a chicken
with someone who tells jokes ?

A comedihen !
or
Lenny Henry !

What do you get if you cross a cricketer
with a hat ?

Two bowlers !

What do you get if you cross a
football team with ice cream ?

Aston Vanilla !

What do you get if you cross
hockey equipment with
hiking gear ?

A pucksack !

What do you get if you cross a pig with a
mathematical quantity ?

A pork pi !

What do you get if you cross a goldfish
bowl with a TV ?

Tele-fish-ion !

What do you get if you cross an explorer
with a cat ?

Christopher Colompuss !

What do you get if
you cross a cowboy
with a dinosaur ?

Tyrannosaurus Tex !

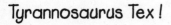

What do you get if you cross a pudding
with an ape ?

Lemon meringue-utan pie !

What do you get if you cross a river with a broken bridge ?

Very wet I should think !

★

What do you get if you cross a tree with a fruit ?

A Pineapple !

★

What do you get if you cross a maths teacher with anything ?

A maths teacher !

What do you get if you cross a pony with a TV detective ?

Inspector Horse !

What do you get if you cross a
cow pat and a microprocessor ?

A com-pooh-ter !

What do you get if you cross a mouse
and an elephant ?

An animal that's scared to look in the mirror !

What do you get if
you cross a dog
with someone
worried about
something ?

Nervous Rex !

What do you get if you cross a duck and
a TV programme ?

A Duckumentary !

What do you get if you cross two rows of cabbages with a main road?

A dual cabbageway !

What do you get if you cross kitchen equipment with a vampire ?

Count spatula !

What do you get if you cross a giant ape with an aeroplane ?

King Kongcorde !

What do you get if you cross a cat and an octopus ?

A cat-o-nine-tails !

What do you get if you cross a farm worker
with some cheese and pickle ?

A ploughman's lunch !

What do you get if you cross a
pop group with a ton of latex ?

A rubber band !

What do you get if you cross a cow pat with a
boomerang ?

A nasty smell you can't get rid of !

What do you get if you cross dandruff
and a French fried potato ?

A chip on your shoulder !

What do you get if you cross a stick of
dynamite and a pig ?

Bangers !

What do you get if you
cross a giraffe
and a cow ?

**Something you need a
ladder to milk !**

What do you get if you
cross a traffic warden
with a dog ?

A barking ticket !

What do you get if you cross a coal mine
with a cow ?

A pit - bull !

What do you get if you cross a cow with
a CD player ?

Pop - Moosic !

What do you get if you mislay your violin
in a match factory ?

Fiddlesticks !

What do you get if you cross a fox
with a carrot ?

Something that no rabbit will dare to steal from the
vegetable patch !

What do you get if you cross a pantomime actor with an opera singer ?

The panto of the opera !

Oh, No you don't...

Oh, yes you do...

Oh, no you don't...

What do you get if you cross a box of hankies with a cold ?

A - A - A -tishoo !

What do you get if you cross a glove puppet with a mouse ?

Sooty and squeak !

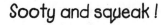

What game do you get if you cross
frogs legs and whisky ?

Hop scotch !

What do you get if you cross a scary
story and a dog ?

Someone who is terrier - fied !

What do you get if you cross a ghost
and a garden party ?

A fete worse than death !

What do you get if you
cross the X files with something you keep your fuel in ?

A coal Scully !

What do you get if you cross a window with
a guillotine ?

A pane in the neck !

★

What do you get if
you cross a carrier
pigeon and a
woodpecker ?

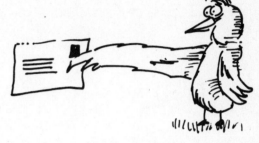

A bird that knocks
before delivering the
message !

★

What do you get if you cross a pig with an
expensive car ?

A sausage roller !

★

What do you get if you cross a James Bond movie
and a footballer ?

Goal - finger !

What do you get if you cross the Radio Times with a microchip ?

Lots of computer programmes on TV !

What do you get if you cross a heavy goods vehicle and an ice cream ?

An articulated lolly !

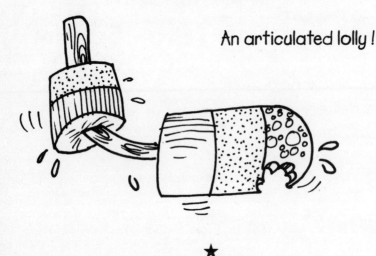

What do you get if you cross a film director and a horse drawn vehicle ?

Orson Kart !

★

What do you get if you cross
a spy and a duvet ?

An under-cover agent !

What do you get if you
cross a ghost
and an optician ?

Spook - tacles !

What do you get if you cross a giant
monopoly set with a safari guide ?

A big game hunter !

What do you get if
you cross a man
inside your TV set and
someone very brainy ?

In - tele - gent !

What do you get when
teenage aliens have a
party ?

A space racket !

★

What do you get if you
cross a policeman
and a tree ?

Special Branch !

★

What do you get if you cross a vampire and a boat ?

A blood vessel !

★

What do you get if you
draw dots and dashes
on your hanky ?

A code in the nose !

What do you get if you cross a spot, a man
who saved peoplefrom
the guillotine and a tin of red paint ?

The Scarlet Pimple !

What do you get if you
cross a dog
with a tree ?

**Something with
a completely
silent bark !**

What do you get if you cross a French and a German
fortune telling device ?

A oui - ja board !

What do you get if you cross a TV detective and
Darth Vader ?

Inspector Force !

What do you get if you cross
a field with some cows in it ?

A pat on the shoe !

What do you get if you
cross a postman, cow dung,
a tap on the head and a
small piece of butter, and
the whole thing sounds
like an outboard engine... ?

Pat, pat, pat, pat...!

What do get when
you cross an angry
young man and someone
who can't decide
which of his 20 shoes
to wear ?

a ten pair tantrum !

What do you get if you
cross cats and
dogs and put them in
cars ?

Datsun cogs !

★

What do you get if you cross a painting and
a rodent ?

A mouse - terpiece !

★

What do you get if you cross the African
jungle with a map of Manchester ?

Completely lost !

★

What do you get if you
cross a portable stereo
and a pig ?

A Porkman !

What do you get if you cross a
footballer with a ghost ?

A Ghoul keeper !

What do you get if you cross an
angry rabbit and an oven ?

A hot cross bun !

What do you get if you cross
a dog with a scientist ?

Something in a Lab coat !

What do you get if you cross
two vampire
red Indians ?

Blood brothers !

Awful Alphabet

ALLOCATE

Allocate - *Say hello to Kate!*

A

Abandon - When a pop group is playing !

Abrade - A Chinese knife !

Accident - When you cut yourself chopping firewood !

Address - Something a woman wears at her wedding !

Adorn - A beautiful start to the day !

Aftermath - The result of a catastrophe - is where we get the word maths !

Airliner - The person who paints the lines down the side of Jumbo jets!

ALLOCATE

Allocate - Say hello to Kate !

Antelope - When two ants run off to get married !

Antifreeze - When your Mum's sister goes out without a coat in Winter !

Arrest - What a burglar gets when he goes to bed !

Automate - A robot for a best pal !

B

Bacteria - The rear entrance to a cafeteria !

Bandage - The average age of a pop group !

Banshee - Don't let that ghost in here !

Barber - Sheep trained as a hairdresser !

Bark - The sound made by a wooden dog !

Bateau - What the French use to play tenniso, squasho and cricketo !

Batman - The secret identity of Dracula !

Beauty Spot - When flowers grow out of your head !

Berth - Where they keep any babies born at sea !

Beverage - Slightly worse than average !

Beware - What bees wear, of course !

Bichromate - A friend you go cycling with !

C

Cabbage - How old a taxi is !

Cagoule - Ghost who goes around in a car !

Canary Islands - Where cats like to go for their holidays !

Candidate - The sweets you take to impress a new girlfriend !

Capacity - The size of your head !

Carousel - A used car dealership !

Carrot - Rust !

Chemistry - The tree you end up in when the lab explodes !

Chipmunk - Chef in a monastery !

Clay Pigeon - School dinners !

Commentator - Any potato that isn't a Jersey Royal or King Edward !

Crime Wave - Where robbers go to surf !

Czech - Money paid into a foreign bank account !

D

Debate - De thing on de fish hook !

Defeatist - Someone who designs shoes !

Demijohn - Robin Hood's best friend !

Dentist - Car body repairer !

Descant - Ant that lives in a school !

Desert - Pudding made from sand !

Detention - The fear of being kept behind at school !

Diplomat - A mat for kneeling on when you meet a V.I.P. !

Discount - How much a shop assistant will knock off a new CD player 'cos he's no good at maths !

Distressed - Having all your hair cut off !

Dynamo - Welshman refusing to cut the grass !

E

Earring - Answer the telephone !

Eclipse - Hedge cutter !

Editor - Policeman's truncheon !

Eider - Not bothered !

Einstein - One glass of beer !

Elastic Band - A group who play rubber instruments !

Electrocute - Pretty electrician !

Engineers - Ears on an engine

Extension - More stress caused by a longer exam !

F

Factory - The place where they make trees !

Falter - Give a girl low marks in a test !

Fax - The truth !

Feedback - A baby being sick !

Fez - Nickname for a pheasant !

Fiddlesticks - Violin bows !

Figure Head - Someone who is good at maths !

Finishing School - The start of the Summer holidays !

Fish and chips - What they serve in the canteen of a nuclear power station !

Flash bulb - A light bulb that thinks very highly of itself !

Footnote - When you try to hide a five pound note with your shoe, until no-one is looking and you can pick it up !

Frankincense - The man who runs the perfume shop !

PERFUME

G

Game keeper - The teacher who confiscates your
Nintendo !

Gazette - Baby Gazelle !

Germinate - Bacteria in bad food !

Genealogy - Finding out if there is a genie in your
family history !

Glacier - The cold stare of the man fixing the
windows you smashed with your football !

Gymkhana - The owner of the local riding school !

H

Hail stones - Over cooked water droplets !

Hallmarks - Black skid marks on the corridor you make as you screech to a halt when a teacher comes round the corner suddenly !

Handiwork - A job just around the corner from where you live !

Hatchback - A car full of baby chicks !

Headrest - Lunch time !

Heirloom - When someone leaves you a pet rabbit in their will !

Hemlock - Special stitch used around the bottom of a skirt !

Highway Code - What hitch hikers catch from standing about in the rain !

Hippodrome - Where hippos go to learn to fly !

Honey comb - What bees use to style their hair !

Hot Cross Bun - What you get if you pour boiling
water down a rabbit hole !

I

Ice lolly - What they use for money at the North Pole !

Icicle - A bicycle with a bit missing !

Ideogram - Telegram sent to an idiot !

Ignite - Eskimo's bedtime !

Impatient - Someone fidgeting in the doctor's waiting room !

Implicate - Blame Kate for something she didn't do !

Infant - Baby elephant !

Infantry - Army made up of baby elephants !

Infiltrate - Sneaking Phil into the football match without paying !

Instep - The latest dance !

Instrumental - Driven crazy by next door's piano lessons !

J

Jackdaw - Small entrance for birds found in a tree !

Jam packed - A very full sandwich !

Jargon - Stolen jar !

Jitterbug - Insect that can't sit still !

Joan of Arc - Noah's wife !

Jodhpurs - Trousers worn by a cat !

Juggernaut - Empty jug !

K

Kaleidoscope - Bump into people while you're looking through a telescope !

Ketchup - Run as fast as a bottle of sauce !

Kettle drum - What the orchestra uses to make a cup of tea !

Kipper - Sleeping fish !

Knickers - Burglars !

Knit wear - Jumper for a fool !

L

Labrador - Dog that helps a scientist with his experiments !

Lacewing - Where prisoners make lace !

Lactose - Monster with ends of feet cut off !

Lambda - Greek letter invented by a sheep !

Lamination - Country ruled by sheep !

Lassitude - Monster eats girl !

Laughing Stock - What you get if you tickle an Oxo cube !

Launderette - A small launder - but I've no idea what a launder is !?

Leek - Vegetable that is not allowed on a boat !

Lemonade - What you give a deaf orange !

Leopard Lilly - A plant you should never sniff !

Level Headed - What you will be if someone drops a car on your head !

Lie Detector - What sneaky teachers use to see who is asleep in the class !

Light Fingered - Someone who steals bulbs !

Lockjaw - What you are likely to get if you swallow a bunch of keys !

Logarithm - Music played by pieces of wood !

Loose Leaf Folder - Where to store all the fallen Autumn leaves !

Luke warm - What Luke is every winter because he manages to sit next to the only radiator in the class room !

Luminous - Toilets that glow in the dark !

M

Macintosh - Waterproof Computer !

Magician - Anyone who can score more than 14% in a maths examination !

Magneto - Italian for magnet !

Mammoth - Large hairy moth with tusks - now extinct !

Manure - What some odd people put on their rhubarb - I put custard on mine !

Marionette - Marion's little sister !

Marksman - Teacher with exam results file !

Marxist - Someone who watches old Marx Brothers films all day !

Melancholy - What you get if you cross a sheep dog with a fruit !

Mental Block - When someone stands in front of the door in the exam room to stop you escaping!

Metacarpus - Scene of an accident involving a motor vehicle and a cat!

Metronome - Short person working on the Paris underground railway system!

Minimum - Metronome's mother!

Mumbo Jumbo - Elephant who doesn't speak clearly !

MUMBLE...
MUTTER...

Mushroom - The room where all the Eskimos go to train their husky dogs to pull sleds. You will often hear the word 'mush' as you walk past !

Mute - A Lute without any strings !

N

Nag - Tell off a horse !

Nappy - Liable to fall asleep in History lessons !

Negligent - Man in a nightie !

Newsagent - Spy hiding behind a newspaper !

Nickname - Put someone else's name on your exam
paper !

Nightmare - Horse that can only be ridden during the hours of darkness !

Nipper - Baby crab !

Nose Cone - Trip up and splat the end of your ice cream into your face !

Nuclear Fuel - Someone who messes around in a power station !

O

Oblique - The feeling you get at the start of a three hour maths exam !

Oblong - The feeling you get when you have finished all the questions and it is still only half way through a three hour maths exam !

Octangle - The feeling an octopus gets in a three hour maths exam !

Offenbach - Noisy dog !

Offensive - Garden fence that nobody likes !

Opt out - Leave the sports field because of a damaged foot !

Orchid - Baby orchestra !

Orienteering - Trying to find your way to Asia with out a map or compass !

Outcrop - That little tuft of hair that the barber always seems to miss !

Outnumber - Finally leaving that three hour maths exam !

P

Padlocks - handcuffs for cats and dogs !

Pamphlet - Leaflet written by Pam !

Pant - Half a pair of trousers !

Paranoid - Robot who is convinced that someone is out to get him !

Parasite - Where leeches go on their Summer holiday !

Parking Meter - Space for a very, very short car !

Parrot Fashion - What trendy parrots wear !

Part Exchange - Transplant surgery !

Party Wall - What neighbours bang on when you make too much noise !

Pas de Deux - Less than 2% in the French Exam !

Picket - What you do when your nose goes on strike !

Pigment - Special paint for colouring pigs !

Q

Quadrangle - Fight in the school playground !

Quadratic Equation - Maths problem that you need
at least 4 people to solve !

Quasimodo - Don't remember the name, but the
face rings a bell !

Quicksilver - Easily spent pocket money !

R

Raquet - Noise made by tennis players !

Rainbow - What the rain wears in its hair !

Ransome - Only completed part of the school cross country race !

Ransome Note - A letter that someone gives the teacher to tell him that you only ran part of the cross country !

Ratbag - Mouse's rucksack!

Ray Gun - Previous President of the United States!

Recycle - Do up an old bike!

Rehearse - Drive back to the graveyard!

Remainder - All the numbers you are left with at the end of the maths exam!

Reverse Charge - Who you telephone to stop a herd of wild elephants!

Roller Skate - Sea fish with his own wheels !

Rosette - Small rose !

Royal Blue - When the Queen is fed up !

Rubber Tree - What they use to make those pencils with an eraser at the end !

Rustle - Paper boy !

S

Salad Dressing - What you will see salad do when it gets up in the morning !

Sand Bank - Where camels keep their savings !

Satire - Sitting in a tall chair !

Scatter Cushions - Result of a pillow fight !

Scholastic - What holds up your P.E. shorts !

Schumaker - cobbler !

Scissors - Swimming leg action designed to cut
through the water !

Scotch Egg - What you get if you feed chickens whisky !

Scrunch - Lunchbox run over by a bus !

Sea Horse - What the idiot bought because he
wanted to play water polo !?

Semiconductor - Part time bus driver !

Shamrock - A plant pretending to be a stone !

Sheba - Queen with a lot of sheep !

Sheep Dip - What wolves have at parties !

Sheep Dog Trial - What happens after sheep dogs are arrested !

Sheet Lightning - What happens if lightning hits your bed !

Shellfish - Crustaceans that never share anything !

Shingle - How a drunk asks for one !

Shortbread - A loaf cut in half !

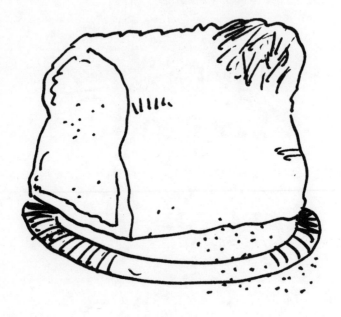

Spell Checker - Computer software for witches !

T

Tactical - Tickling a small nail !

Tap Dancer - Someone trying to do River Dance in the sink !

Telethon - Well, Thwitch it off then Thilly !

Tinfoil - Not very thick foil !

Tirade - Robbery in a tie shop !

Toadstool - Hammer belonging to a toad !

Toulouse - Two toilets !

Track Suit - What a railway line wears when it goes out jogging !

Traffic Jam - What policemen have in their sandwiches !

Tycoon - Someone who has made a lot of money selling ties !

U

Ultimatum - When you tell your friend for the last time !

Umpire - Vampire who can't spell !

Unaware - Boxer shorts !

Undecided - Not knowing what colour unaware
to put on !

Underpass - Handing secret notes under your desk !

Underrate - Any number from 1 to 7

Unit - Fool !

University - Training school for poets !

Unleaded - Empty pencil case !

Unstable - Horse that lives in a field !

V

Vacuum Cleaner - Used to keep outer space nice and tidy !

Vague - (Sorry, not sure about this one !)

Vampire - Where you go to hire a vamp !

Varnish - A posh way of disappearing !

Vespers - Very quiet whispers !

Vest - opposite to East !

W

Waist Coat - Jacket made from scraps of material !

Wardrobe - Cupboard that joins the army !

Warhead -
Head
teacher
who joins
the army !
Hurrah !

Warren -
A man who
keeps pet
rabbits !

Weight Watcher - Someone who spends a lot of time
looking at their tum !

X - Y - Z

X-Ray - Used to belong to Ray!

Xylophone - What aliens from the planet Xylo use to telephone each other!

Yak - What you say when you stand in something nasty!

Yam - How they say Jam in Holland!

Yardstick - Sweeping brush with a missing head!

Yellow Hammer - What you shout when you hit your thumb !

Yellow Pages - Homework book with tea spilled on it !

Yoga - Cartoon bear !

Yokel - Farmworker who paints egg yolks yellow !

Zebra - Mobile road crossing !

Zermatt - What you wipe zer feet on !

Zinc - Where you wash your hands !

Zing - What you do with zongs in a choir !

Zoo - What a solicitor does !

Zoom Lens - The sound of a camera falling from a
great height !

Zulu – The toilets in the zoo !

Hospital Howlers

Doctor, doctor...
What can I do to help me get to sleep ?

Have you tried counting sheep ?

Yes, but then I have to wake up to drive
home again !

Why did the angry doctor have to retire ?

Because he had lost all his patients !

Doctor, doctor...
I think I've got an inferiority complex !

No you haven't - you really are inferior !

Ah. Mr Smith, have your eyes ever been checked ?

No doctor, they've always been blue !

★

Doctor, doctor...
There's a man to see you with a wooden leg
called Jenkins.

What's his other leg called ?

★

Doctor, doctor...
I think I'm turning into a
wasp !

**Hmm , give me a buzz if
things get really bad !**

★

Doctor, doctor...
I've just been stung by a
wasp !

Did you put anything on it ?

**No, he seemed to enjoy it
just as it was !**

★

Doctor, doctor...
I've got an itchy spotty patch on my nose,
should I put cream on it ?

Now, now, let's not do anything rash !

Doctor, doctor...
I've not stopped laughing since my operation !

Well, I told you the surgeon would have you in stitches !

Doctor, doctor...
I've got pigeon toes !

**Don't worry we'll find a suitable tweetment for you...
but for now just put this birdseed in your shoes !**

★

Doctor, doctor...
My belly is so big I'm embarrassed by it !

Have you tried to diet ?

Yes, but whatever colour I use it still sticks out !

★

Doctor's Bookcase...

TRAINING TO BE A SURGEON

by

I. CUTTEM - OPEN

Doctor, doctor...
I feel like a twenty pound note !

Go shopping, the change will do you good !

Doctor, doctor...
I can't stop shoplifting !

Try taking two of these pills every morning,
and if that doesn't work bring me
a CD player next week !

Doctor, doctor...
Did you hear about the appendix who
went out and bought a new suit -
because he heard that the doctor was
going to take him out !

Doctor, doctor...
Which king was also a doctor ?

William the corn curer !

Doctor, doctor...
Is it true that you can get pills to improve your memory?

Of course you can, how many would you like?

How many what?

Doctor, doctor...
Which kings needed medical attention?

**Charles the sick
and
Henry the ache!**

★

Doctor, doctor...
I feel as sick as a dog !

I'll make an appointment for you to see a vet !

Doctor, doctor...
Thank you for coming - I'm at death's door !

Don't worry, I'll pull you through !

Doctor, doctor...
I keep thinking I'm a big bar of chocolate !

Come and sit here, and don't worry, I won't bite - I'm
just a big old pussycat really !

Doctor, doctor...
I've got a terrible cough !

Well you should practice more !

Doctor, doctor...
After the operation on my hand
will I be able to play the piano ?
Of course you will Mr Smith !

Great - because I never could before !

Doctor, doctor...
my son is turning into a cricket bat !

Hmm ! Well, this has got me stumped !

Doctor, doctor...
I think I'm turning into a fish !

Well, just hop up on to the scales !

Doctor, doctor...
I feel like a goat !

Really - and how are the kids ?

★

Doctor, doctor...
I think I'm turning into a bridge !

Really - what's come over you ?

Doctor, doctor...
Why did the chemist tell everyone to be quiet?

Because she didn't want to wake the sleeping pills !

Doctor, doctor...
These tablets you gave me last week seem
to get smaller every day ?!

Yes, they're slimming pills !

Doctor, doctor...
I think I'm turning into a toad !

**Don't worry, we can do an hoperation
for that these days !**

Doctor, doctor...
Can you put me in touch with the local
plastic surgeon ?

**I'm afraid not, he sat too close to the
radiator last night and melted !**

Doctor, doctor...
I have a fish hook stuck in the side of my mouth !

**I thought you were waiting to see me
with baited breath !**

★

Doctor, doctor...
I've just been stung by a giant wasp !

I'll give you some cream to put on it !

Don't be daft - it'll be miles away by now !

★

Doctor, doctor...
My new job at the laundry is very tiring !

I thought you looked washed out !

Ah, Mr Blenkinsop. Did you drink the medicine
I gave you after your bath ?

**No, Doctor, I couldn't even drink all the bath
let alone the medicine !**

Doctor, doctor...
I get a lot of headaches from my wooden leg.

Why is that ?

**Because my wife keeps hitting me
over the head with it !**

Doctor, doctor...
I think I have a split personality !

I'd better give you a second opinion then !

★

Doctor, doctor...
I got trampled by a load of cows !

So I herd !

Doctor, doctor...
I keep imagining I,m a sunken ship and it's
really got me worried !

Sounds to me like you're a nervous wreck !

Doctor, doctor...
My snoring wakes me up every night !

**Try sleeping in another bedroom, then you
won't be able to hear it !**

Doctor, doctor...
I feel quite like my old self again !

Oh Dear, I better put you back on the tablets then !

Doctor, doctor...
My hair is falling out - can you give me something to keep it in ?

Here's a paper bag ?!

Doctor, doctor...
What can you give me for my kidneys ?

How about a pound of onions ?!

Doctor, doctor...
I've fractured my elbow bone !

Humerus ?

Well, I don't think it's particularly funny !

Doctor, doctor...
Is this disease contagious?

Not at all!

Then why are you standing out on the window ledge?!

Doctor, doctor...
You don't really think I'm turning into a
grandfather clock do you?

No, I was just winding you up!

Doctor, doctor...
I think I have acute appendicitis!

Yes, it is rather nice isn't it!

Doctor, doctor, I have an inferiority complex!

Hmm. Not a very big one is it!

Doctor, doctor, I think I'm a pair of curtains!

Pull yourself together!

Doctor, doctor, my wife thinks she's a motorbike!

Give her two of these pills and she'll be cured!

But how will I get home then?

Doctor, doctor, I'm shrinking!

Well, you'll just have to be a little patient!

Doctor, doctor, my wife
thinks she's a chicken!

Do you want me to
cure her?

No. I just wondered
if you had any good
egg recipes!

Doctor, doctor, everyone
keeps ignoring me!

Next patient please!

Doctor, doctor, I think I'm a pack of cards!

You'll just have to deal with it yourself!

Doctor, doctor, I think I'm a mousetrap!

Snap out of it!

Doctor, doctor, all my friends think I'm a liar !

I find that hard to believe !

Doctor, doctor, I keep thinking that my
parents are goats !

When did you start to have these thoughts ?

When I was a kid !

I SENT
HIM
HOME
TO
FETCH
HIS
NANNY!

Doctor, doctor, I think I'm becoming invisible !

I'm sorry, I can't see you now !

Doctor, doctor, I have a lot of wind, can you give me anything for it ?

Certainly, here's a kite !

★

Doctor, doctor, you know those pills you gave me for a headache - well they worked. Now can you give me something to take the headache away !

★

Doctor, doctor, I think I'm a billiard ball !

Sorry, you'll have to go to the end of the cue !

★

PARDON ME !

Doctor, doctor, I keep thinking I'm a roll of film !

Don't worry, I'm sure nothing will develop !

★

Nurse, nurse, I need to see a doctor !

Which doctor?

No, just an ordinary one !

HE'S PAYING !

★

Doctor, doctor, I think I have a split personality !

In that case I will have to charge you double !

★

Doctor, doctor, I'm a little hoarse !

I'll be with you in a minute - just take your saddle off and relax !

Doctor, doctor, I swallowed a spoon !

Just sit there quietly and don't stir !

Doctor, doctor, I've lost my memory !

That's terrible. When did you first notice ?

When did I notice what ?

Doctor, doctor, I think I'm a dog !

Well, fetch this stick then roll over and let me tickle your tummy !

Will that cure me ?

No, but I was never allowed to have a pet as a child !

Doctor, doctor, my wife wants to know if you can stop me being so argumentative ?

I'm sorry Mr. Brown, there's nothing I can do !

Yes there is !

Doctor, doctor, I'm not feeling myself today, so can you ask the doctor to call round and see Mr. Smith instead !

Doctor, doctor, I keep thinking that I have been here before !

Oh. It's you again !

Doctor, doctor, can you help me to stop smoking ?

Well, you could try not setting fire to your trousers !

Doctor, doctor, I've just swallowed a tin
of gloss paint !

**Yes, my receptionist said you'd taken a
shine to her !**

★

Doctor, doctor my wife just buried
my radio in the garden !

Why did she do that ?

The batteries were dead !

Doctor, doctor, I've got
athlete's foot
in my head !

What makes you
think that ?

**Because my nose
keeps running !**

★

Doctor, doctor, what's the best cure for water on the knee?

A tap on the ankle!

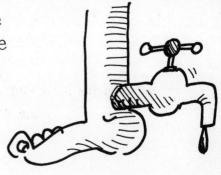

Doctor, doctor, I have flowers growing out of the top of my head!

Don't worry, it's just a beauty spot!

Doctor, doctor, I think I need glasses!

I'll say you do - this is a fish and chip shop!

★

Doctor, doctor, I'm suffering from delusions of grandeur!

Sit down, your Majesty, and tell me all about it!

Doctor, doctor, I'm covered in spots - I need to do something about it straight away !

Now, now, let's not do anything rash !

Doctor, doctor, my dog has just bitten me !

In that case we will need to check for infection !

Thank you - that will put my mind at rest !

So, when can you bring the dog in?

Doctor, doctor, I kissed a girl and she turned into a frog !

Where is she now ?

Waiting in the croakroom !

Doctor, doctor I can't stop sneezing -
what can you give me ?

A tissue ?

Oh, no, it's happening to you as well now !

Doctor, doctor, I'm worried. This is the first time I've
had an operation !

I know how you feel - it's the first time I've done one !

Doctor, doctor, I get so nervous when I drive I keep
bumping into things !

Don't worry I'll prescribe a crash course !

Doctor, doctor I've gone blind,
what should I do ?

Put your crash helmet on the right way round !

Doctor, doctor, the chemist says these pills you prescribed me are for cows !

Well, you said you wanted to be as strong as an ox !

Doctor, doctor, I keep seeing numbers in front of my eyes all the time !

Take two of these pills every night !

Will I ever be cured ?

I wouldn't count on it !

Doctor, doctor, I keep seeing spots
in front of my eyes !

Have you seen an optician !

No, just the spots !

Doctor, doctor, there's a rumour going round that
you're a vampire !

Nonsense ! Necks please !

Doctor, doctor, wherever I
go I hear this ringing
in my ears !

**I'm not surprised, you
always wear
bell bottoms !**

Doctor, doctor, I think I have a split personality !

I'm sorry, one of you will have to wait outside !

Doctor, doctor, I think I'm a pack of cards !

You'll just have to play patients for a while !

Doctor, doctor, why are you so short tempered ?

I don't have enough patients !

Doctor, doctor, three beer kegs have
just fallen on me ?

Don't worry, it was light ale !

Doctor, doctor, I think I'm turning
into a mummy !

Hmmm. better keep well wrapped up !

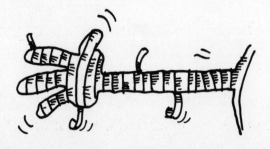

Doctor, doctor, I think I need some antibiotics!

Why, are you feeling ill?

No, but my auntie feels terrible!

Doctor, doctor, I think I've caught a computer virus!

I've warned you before about eating chips!

Doctor, doctor, I've started having dizzy spells!

When do they start?

Whenever I step off the roundabout!

Doctor, doctor, I have these little flowers growing out of my feet !

It's all right, they're just corn flowers !

Doctor, doctor, my husband has gone all furry, and he smells of mints all the time !

This could be serious, sounds like he's turning into a polo bear !

Doctor, doctor, I've lost my memory !

Well, Mr Smith, if you would like to pay the outstanding £10,000 from your last bill I'll have a look at you !

Nurse, nurse, will the doctor be around soon ?

No, he'll be tall and slim as usual !

Doctor, doctor, I'm an insomniac !

Don't worry, we treat everyone
regardless of their religion !

Doctor, doctor, I'm scared, this is my first operation !

Yeah ! Me too !

Doctor, doctor, my husband keeps dressing
up like a French soldier !

Another case of legionnaires disease !

Doctor, doctor, I need you to recommend
a good plastic surgeon !

Why, what do you need done ?

**Well, I put the TV too close to the fire
and it's melted !**

Doctor, doctor, I just know that you can help me with
my flat feet !

What do you want me to do ?

**Just reverse your car off them and they
would be a lot better !**

Doctor, doctor, I'm suffering
from terrible insomnia!

**Oh! I'm sure all you need is a
good night's sleep!**

Doctor, doctor, can you help
me to lose weight?

Well, you could lose 20 kilos straight away!

How on earth do I do that?

Put down those shopping bags!

Doctor, doctor, I've just
swallowed 70 pence?

Why on earth did you
do that!

**I was feeling ill, and I
thought the change
would do me good!**

Doctor, doctor, I've just been bitten by a snake - do you think there is any chance of an infection?

I wouldn't have thought so, snakes are pretty resilient creatures!

Doctor, doctor, my snoring is driving my neighbours crazy!

Well, maybe you should sleep in your own home from now on!

★

Doctor, doctor, my pig has pimples, what should I give him?

Try this oinkment!

★

Doctor, doctor, I only have one tooth, what should I do?

You'll just have to grin and bare it!

Gruesome Giggles

Why did the skull go to the disco
on his own ?

He had no body to go with !

What do monsters eat for breakfast ?

Human beans on toast !

★

How many skeletons can you fit in an empty coffin ?

Just one - after that it's not empty any more !

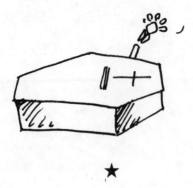

★

What did the mummy ghost say to the little ghost ?

Don't spook until you're spooken to !

★

Where would you find a suitable gift for
a tortured ghost ?

In a chain store !

Why did the vampire bite a computer?

He wanted to get onto the interneck!

What day of the week do vampires and werewolves like best?

Moonday - especially full-moonday!

What sort of ghost would you find up your nose?

A Bogeyman!

How do you know if there is a ghost in a hotel ?

Ask to see the hotel in - spectre !

Why should you never run if you see a werewolf ?

Because they go mad for fast food !

What sort of music do ghosts like best ?

Haunting melodies !

How do mummies go into their pyramids ?

Gift wrapped !

Why did the zombie go to the chemists ?

He wanted something to stop his coffin !

What should you never order if you're
eating out with a vampire ?

Steak and chips !

EEK!

What is a ghosts' favourite creature ?

The Whale !

Why do ghosts go back to the same place
every year for their holidays ?

They like their old haunts best !

Vampire Hunters Menu...

GARLIC BREAD

followed by

HAMMERED STEAK

and finally

HOT CROSS BUNS

What do you call a ghost that doesn't scare anyone ?

A failure !

What does a well-brought-up vampire say
after he has bitten your neck ?

Fang you very much !

VAMPIRE SAYINGS...

Once bitten - twice bitten !

A neck in your hand is worth two in a bush !

A stitch in time - means I can come back for some more !

There's many a slip twixt neck and lip !

What is a skeleton ?

A body with the person scraped off !

★

What does a skeleton feed his dog ?

Anything but bones !!

★

Why do skeletons take a dog with them to the seaside ?

They need something to bury them in the sand !

Why do skeletons drink lots of milk ?

Because calcium is good for your bones !

Why was the skeleton's jacket in shreds ?

Because he had very sharp shoulder blades !

Why do skeletons dislike horror films ?

Because they scare them to the marrow !

What sort of jokes do skeletons enjoy ?

Rib ticklers !

What do skeletons sing at birthday parties ?

Femur jolly good fellow. . .

What do skeletons eat on Good Friday ?

Hot Cross Bones !

What do skeleton schoolchildren wear ?

Knee caps !

What do vampires eat at parties ?

Fang Furters !

What do you call a very old vampire ?

A Gran-pire !

How do vampires and ghosts go on holiday ?

By Scareyplane !

What did the teacher say to the naughty vampires in class ?

Stop Dracularking about !

Did you hear about the ghost who cut down trees at three o'clock in the morning ?

He was the thing that made stumps in the night !

What do you call twin ghosts ?

Dead ringers !

★

Why was the vampire lying dead on the floor of the restaurant ?

It was a steak house !

What does a young boy ghost do to get a girlfriend ?

He wooooooooos her !

What are the only jobs that skeletons can get ?

Skeleton staff !

What about the two ghosts who got married -
it was love at first fright !

What do ghosts do if they are afraid ?

Hide under a sheet !

What is the difference between a ghost
and a custard cream biscuit ?

Have you tried dipping a ghost in your tea ?!

How does a skeleton know when it's
going to rain ?

He just gets a feeling in his bones !

What is ... visible - invisible - visible - invisible -
visible - invisible ?

A skeleton on a zebra crossing !

Where do vampires get washed ?

In the bat room !

What room must all werewolf homes have ?

A changing room !

What sort of shampoo do ghosts use ?

Wash and Groan !

What do you call a vampire that hides in the kitchen ?

Spatula !

GHASTLY GHOSTLY SAYINGS. . .

Two's company - threes a shroud !

Never kick a ghost while he's down -
your foot will just go through him !
**He who laughs last - obviously hasn't
seen the ghost standing behind him !**

What do ghosts watch on TV ?

Scare Trek !

Horror Nation Street !

Bone and Away !

The Booos at Ten !

Sesame Sheet !

Have I got whoooos for you !

and, of course...

Till Death Us Do Part !

What can you use to flatten a ghost ?
A spirit level !

Why did the ghosts have a party ?

They wanted to lift their spirits !

What do ghosts carry their luggage in
when they go on holiday ?

Body bags !

SKELEMENU...

Ox-Tail Soup

followed by

Spare Ribs and Finger Buffet

finishing with

Marrowbone Jelly and Custard !

What do skeletons learn about at school?

Decimals and Fractures!

Where does a vampire keep his money?

In a blood bank!

What do you call an overweight vampire?

Draculard!

What do you call a vampire mummy?

Wrapula!

What do you call a young vampire ?

Draculad !

What do you call a vampire that attacks insects ?

A cricket bat !

After the monster had bitten off both my legs the police refused to arrest him !

Why was that ?

They said he had no arm in him !

What's green and hairy and has 18 legs ?

I don't know !

Neither do I, but it's just crawled up into your shorts !

Why did the chicken cross the road?

I don't know!

**It was going for an eye test,
which explains why
it got hit by a bus!**

What did the bus conductor
say to the monster with
3 heads, no arms and 1 leg?

Hello, hello, hello you look armless, hop on!

This oatmeal tastes terrible -
did you wash it before you cooked it?

**I certainly did, and here is
the bar of oatmeal soap
I washed it with!**

Doctor - Stand in front of the window and stick out your tongue.

Patient - Are you going to examine it?

Doctor - No, I just don't like the man who lives in the house opposite!

What do you call a deer with its eyes poked out?

No eye deer!

What do you call a dead deer with its eyes poked out?

Still no eye deer!

Those toffees were nice - but why were they furry ?

My mum sucked them up into the vacuum cleaner !

Why was the monster eating a horse in his bedroom at two in the morning ?

He was having a night mare !

What is green and white and swings through the trees ?

Tarzan's handkerchief !

Why should you always try to stay awake when you are on a train ?

Because trains run over sleepers !

Waiter - why is there a frog in my soup ?

To catch the flies !

Waiter, why have you got your thumb in my soup ?

I have a boil on my thumb and the doctor said I have to keep it warm !

What's the best thing to do with a green monster ?

Wait until he's ripe or you'll get tummy ache after eating him !

Did you hear about the really stupid woodworm ?

It was found dead in a housebrick !

What is black and white and red at the bottom?

A baby zebra with nappy rash!

What climbs up and down bellropes and is wrapped in a plastic bag?

The lunchpack of Notre Dame!

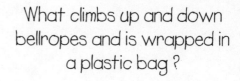

What is black, floats on water and swears?

Crude oil!

A fat man went into the doctors and asked if the doctor had anything to keep his belly in...

...here's a wheelbarrow!

Jim - If there are ten flies on a table and I kill one with a newspaper, how many will be left ?

Joe - Only the dead one !

Who is that at the door ?

A man with a wooden leg.

Tell him to hop it !

Did you hear about the man with two wooden legs who caught fire ?

He burned down to the ground !

A little boy took a bucket into the living room and put it down in front of his elderly granny. He asked her to kick it - "cos then my dad says we'll have plenty of money and I can have a new bike !"

Did you hear about the explorer
who escaped from the cannibals ?

It cost him an arm and a leg !

Doctor - You have four minutes left to live !

Patient - What am I going to do ?

Doctor - **You could boil me an egg ?!**

Did you hear about the man who
stole a lorry load of prunes?

He's been on the run for 6 months!

Mum, do steak pies have legs?

No, dear, of course not!

Oh! Then grandad has just eaten the tortoise!

Why did the jockey take a bale of hay to bed?

To feed his night mares!

Why did the vampire have to go
and see his bank manager?

**He had run up an overdraft on his
blood bank account!**

What is the difference between
a black cloud and someone who has just
had their toes run over?

**One pours with rain
the other roars with pain!**

Waiter - why is there
a dead mouse in my soup?

**You would be dead too
if you'd eaten any of it!**

Waiter, why are there
five pop singers in my soup?

Well, you said you wanted it spicy!

★

What did the doctor give the monster
for his liver ?

A kilo of onions !

What swings through trees backwards ?

Nazrat !

What did the zebra say on the
pedestrian crossing ?

**Now you see me
now you don't
now you see me
now you don't !**

★

'Bring me a large Scotsman,'
said the monster,
'I fancy eating
a Big Mac !'

A 3 legged monster went to the doctor to ask what he could do now that he had had his feet amputated.

You should take up a sport - try cricket - they need 3 stumps !

A monster was looking at his captive humans. He looked at one girl and said 'You look sweet!' The girl smiled, and the monster smiled back. 'OK,' said the monster, 'so that's pudding sorted, now for the main course!'

★

How do you stop a skunk from smelling ?

Cut off it's nose !

★

What do you call a scruffy, unreliable and dishonest individual with no legs ?

A low down bum !

Doctor, doctor, I feel half dead !

Well, I will arrange for you to be buried from the waist down !

★

Mushy Martians

Why did the space monster cover his rocket
with tomato sauce ?

So the nasty aliens couldn't ketchup with him !

Why didn't the Martian have his
birthday party on the Moon ?

There was no atmosphere !

What do astronauts have in
their packed lunch ?

Launcheon Meat !

What is soft and sweet and fluffy
and comes from Mars ?

A Mars-mallow !

What do astronauts wear when it's cold ?

Apollo neck jumpers !

How do you know that Saturn is married ?

You can see the ring !

What game do bored Aliens play ?

Astro noughts and crosses !

What fast food do computers eat ?

Ram Burgers !

What do the aliens from the planet Skunkus ride in ?

Phew F O's !

When the alien picked up his brand new
spaceship he was really pleased –
he'd never had a **NEW F O** before !

★

What sort of spaceships do aliens from the
planet Footwear use ?

Shoe F O's

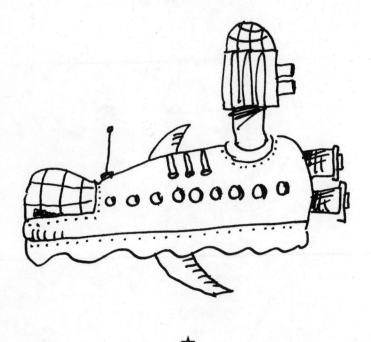

★

How did the space aliens go into the space ark ?

R 2 D 2 by R 2 D 2 !

Alien - Beware Earthling, I could eat your entire planet !

**Blenkinsop - That's nothing, yesterday I ate
an entire Galaxy !**

★

What do you call a pub on Mars ?

A Mars bar !

★

Why did the spaceship land outside your bedroom ?

I must have left the landing light on !

What do you call a space creature that
doesn't pass his space exams ?

A Fail-ien !

What do you get in an alien transport cafe ?

Unidentified frying objects !

What is the smallest space explorer called ?

A Mouse-tronaut !

What do space ramblers like to do ?

Go on Star Treks !

What do you never get if you cross a
bug eyed alien with a dog ?

Burgled !

What is the first thing an alien puts on
when he gets out of bed ?

His feet - ON - the floor !

Where do aliens keep their sandwiches ?

In a launch box !

Why are aliens good gardeners ?

They have green fingers !

Knock, knock...
Who's there ?
Jupiter.
Jupiter who ?
Jupiter space ship on my front lawn ?!

What goes in one year and out the other ?

A time machine !

If astronauts breathe oxygen during the day,
what do they breathe at night ?

Nitrogen !

Knock, knock...
Who's there ?
Saturn.
Saturn who ?
**Saturn front of this spaceship
waiting for take off time !**

What is the weakest part of space called ?

The Punyverse !

What robots are made from small planets ?

Aster - droids !

What do you call a vampire version of Star Trek ?

The Necks Generation !

Human –   Why have you got holes in your hand ?

Alien –   I have been using the computer.

Human –   But that's not dangerous !?

Alien –   **Maybe not on Earth, but on my planet when we talk about computer bytes we mean something different !**

Why do creatures from the planet THaaarRRgh wear slimy green braces ?

To hold their slimy green trousers up !

What do you call a glass robot ?

See through P O !

Why couldn't the moon eat any more supper ?

Because it was full !

What teddy bear story do robot children read at bedtime ?

Tinny - the - Pooh !

What does the alien hairdresser do when the shadow of the earth obscures the sun ?

Eclipse !

How do you get a baby alien to sleep ?

Rocket !

What did the grape say when the space monster trod on him ?

Nothing - he just let out a little whine !

What do you call a noisy space ship ?

A space racket !

What do space aliens watch on TV ?

Countdown !

Why is the letter V like a space monster ?

Because it comes after you !

What do you call the planet that is inhabited
solely by impressionists ?

Planet of the apes !

Which part of a space suit is German ?

The Helmut !

Which Egyptian King was named after a planet ?

Tutankhamoon !

Why are alien kitchens always such a mess ?

Because of all the flying sauces !

What did the tree alien say when he landed on Earth ?

Take me to your Cedar !

What would you do if you saw a spaceman ?

Park in it, man !

Why did the alien buy a twisted spaceship ?

He wanted to travel at warp speed !

Why couldn't the idiot's spaceship travel
at the speed of light ?

Because he took off in the dark !

What do you call dishonest spaceships ?

Lying saucers !

What sort of spaceships do secret agents fly in ?

Spying saucers !

What do you call miserable spaceships ?

Sighing saucers !

Which space villain looks like a pair of wellies ?

Darth Waders !

How often do you find toilets in space ?

Once in a loo moon !

Where do you leave your spaceship whilst you visit
another planet ?

At a parking meteor !

What sort of music do space aliens like best ?

Rocket and roll !

and

Heavy Metal !

Where do they lock up naughty space creatures ?

Jailien !

Why does Captain Kirk make the crew
clean the Enterprise ?

He Likes things Spock and span !

Where do you sometimes hear singing in space ?

When you fly past a pop star !

Why did the alien build a spaceship from feathers ?

He wanted to travel light years !

**Did you hear about the alien poet -
she wrote universes !**

Why did Captain Kirk shave his head ?

To baldly go where no-one had been before !

Did you hear about the silly alien who
built a spaceship from herbs ?

He wanted to travel in thyme !

What do alien footballers wear when
they arrive on Earth ?

Their landing strip !

What piece of sports equipment does every alien own ?

A tennis rocket !

Why did the alien take a nuclear missile to the party ?

In case he fancied blowing up some balloons !

Did you hear about the fat alien - he had to wear a
'not very much' space suit!

How did the moon get a pat on the head ?

When the cow jumped over it !

Space Booklist...

Flying Saucers

by

Hugh Effo

They came from another planet

by

Marsha Nattack

How to build a rubber spaceship

by

Ben D Rocket

What do space monsters call humans ?

Breakfast, Lunch and Dinner !

★

What do aliens do at the disco ?

The Moonwalk !

Where do aliens go to listen to music ?

Nep-tune !

Why do elephants paint themselves silver ?

So they can get a lift by grabbing on to the side of passing spaceships !

Well, I've never seen one do that !

Just shows what a good disguise it is !

What newspaper do aliens read ?

The Sun !

What do you call a spooky alien ?

Extra - terror - estrial !

What did the Martian
~~e~~ from his holiday in outer space ?

Sticks of rocket !

★

How do students have
to sit in robot school ?

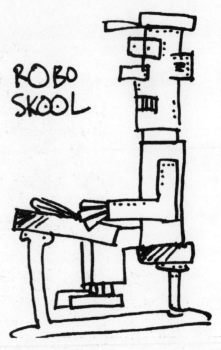

ROBO
SKOOL

Bolt upright !

★

What is a robot's
favourite film ?

Full Metal Jacket !

★

Where do newly-wed Martians go after the service !

On a Honey - Earth !

★

What do you call?

What do you call a Scottish
cloak room attendant?

Willie Angus McCoatup !

What do you call a man with a calculator on
his head ?

Adam !

What do you call a cat that works in a chemists ?

Puss in Boots !

What is a rodent's favourite sport ?

Ka-rat-e !

What do you call someone with a pair of
shoes on their head ?

A sole singer !

What do call a man with 6 arms ?

Andy !

What do call a man with a bowl of custard
on his head ?

Spotted Dick !

What do you call a man with a duck on
his head ?

Quackers !

What do you call a Teddy
that's been
buried in the garden ?

Plan - ted !

What do you call a frog who can leave his
car anywhere ?

A Parking Kermit !

What do you call a man who can sing and drink
lemonade at the same time ?

A pop singer !

What do you call a cat that is always
having accidents ?

A catastrophe !

What do you call a machine for
counting cows ?

A cowculator !

What do you call a robbery in Peking ?

A Chinese take-away !

What do you call the place where sick fairies go ?

The Elf Centre !

What do you call a doctor who works on the M1 ?

A by-pass specialist !

What do you call the man who
writes all Dracula's jokes ?

His crypt writer !

What do you call the
shark who does
impersonations of
one of the Beatles ?

Jaws Harrison !

What do you call work that fairies
have to do after school ?

Gnomework !

What do you call the carpet cleaner
that vampires use ?

A victim cleaner !

What do you call it when your teacher
is having a baby ?

A Miss-conception !

What do you call a spanner belonging
to a toad ?

A toad's tool !

What do you call a man with a
washing machine on his head ?

Otto Matic !

What do you call a Tibetan chicken ?

Himalaya !

What do you call someone who doesn't
use a hanky ?

Greensleeves !

What do you call a prisoner's pet budgie ?

A jailbird !

What do you call it when someone tries to
rob a bank with a bunch of flowers ?

Robbery with violets !

What do you call the largest mouse in the World ?

Hippopotamouse !

What do you call a Teddy bear's favourite drink?

Ginger bear!

What do you call the skeleton who was once the Emperor of France?

Napoleon Boney Parts!

What do you call a cat that works in a hospital?

A first aid kit!

What do you call a cat that plays the drums?

A drum kit!

What do you call a cat that makes models?

A construction kit!

What do you call a snake that grabs a cricketer ?

A bowler constrictor !

★

What do you call the last man
to abandon ship ?

Deaf !

★

What do you call the Elizabethan
explorer who could stop bicycles ?

Sir Francis Brake !

★

What do you call the explorer who was
caught and eaten by cannibals ?

Captain Cooked !

★

What do you call a cat in a panic ?

Cat flap !

What do you call a man with a toilet on his head ?

Lou !

*(Of course he might have two if he
was feeling flush !)*

What do you call twin brothers,
each with a drum on his head ?

Tom, Tom !

What do you call the biggest ant in the World ?

An elephant !

What do you call a house where Martians live ?

A greenhouse !

What do you call the instrument
a skeleton plays ?

A trom - bone !

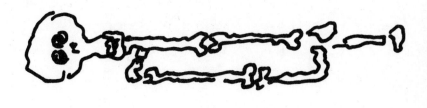

★

What do you call a dog that likes doing experiments ?

A Lab-rador !

★

What do you call the stuff your
milkman delivers if you live at the end of a
two mile cobbled street ?

Yogurt !

★

What do you call the dance where
all cakes are invited ?

Abundance !

What do you call out when
your toadstool bag is
almost full ?

**There's not mushroom
in it now !**

What do you call it when
two cows
munch grass side by side to
keep warm ?

Double grazing !

What do you call a sheep dog when
it has eaten too much melon ?

Melancholy !

What do you call a highly dangerous cake ?

Atilla the bun !

What do you call a cake you eat in the bath ?

Sponge !

What do you call a dog that likes
wrapping presents ?

A boxer !

What do you call a madman who
has a wash then runs away ?

Nut, washes and bolts !

What do you call a homeless snail ?

A slug !

What do you call a chimney built upside down ?

A well !

What do you call the most unhealthy bird ?

The Puffin !

★

What do you call the pliers you use in maths ?

Multipliers !

What do you call spooky
schoolbooks ?

Exorcise books !

★

What do you call stupid flowers that grow
in a pond ?

Water sillies !

What do you call a sheep with fangs ?

A Lamb-pire !

What do you call a the place where aliens
go to see films ?

Cine - Mars !

What do you call a skin complaint
that comes from London ?

Hackney !

What do you call a cat that only knows 9 stories and
bores people to death with them ?

A cat-o-nine-tails !

What do you call a
machine for counting
snakes ?

An adder-ing machine !

What do you call someone
who's been buried for
200 years ?

Peat !

★

What do you call the
Gotham City superheroes
after they have been run
over by a steam roller ?

Flatman and Ribbon !

★

What do you call a
doctor who operates
without anaesthetic on
her nieces and nephews ?

An agony aunt !

★

What do you call the young lady who lives in the coffin
next to dracula's ?

The ghoul next door !

Fishy Folly

Which fish runs the undersea mafia?

The Codfather!

Why are Herrings such healthy fish ?

**Because you never see them ill,
only cured !**

★

What do you call a fish that's always asleep ?

A kipper !

★

*Roses are red,
violets are blue, you
look like a trout, and
you smell like one too !*

★

*If you use a skunk to catch fish you always
catch them hook, line and stinker !*

What do you get in a takeaway next to
a power station ?

Nuclear fission chips !

What do dolphins do when they are late ?

They put their skates on !

Where do dolphins learn ?

In Schools, of course !

Where do baby fish go ?

To Plaice-school !

★

What would you eat in an sunken
pirate ship take-away ?

Pizzas of eight !

How do fish go on holiday?

They take the whale-way!

★

Which sea creatures never go to parties in case they are eaten by mistake?

Jelly fish!

★

Knock, knock...
Who's there?
Plaice...
Plaice who?
**Plaice let me in,
I'm wet through!**

★

Why was the beach wet ?

Because the sea weed !

Why are some shellfish
always bad tempered ?

**They can't help it -
they were
born crabby !**

Where do fish like going for their holidays ?

Finland !

How do fish know exactly
what everything weighs ?

**They always have a set
of scales on them !**

★

What do sharks eat
at parties?

Fish-cakes
Jelly-fish
and
Sandwiches

★

Where do whales get
weighed?

At a whale - weigh station!

★

What do fish drink?

Water of course, they can't use bottle openers!

★

What do fish use to stop
getting sunburned?

Sun tan ocean!

What sort of paintings do fish prefer ?

Watercolours !

Who are the worst criminals in the lake ?

River bank robbers !

What jewellery do lady fish wear ?

Eel-rings !

Which is the strongest sea creature ?

The muscle !

Who does all the woodwork in the sea ?

Plankton !

How do fish pass the long winter evenings ?

They tell each other tails !

What did the sea say to the beach ?

It didn't say anything - it waved !

Where do fish keep their savings ?

In the river bank !

What do you call a whale in the
Sahara desert ?

Lost !

Which part of the fish do we eat that
it doesn't actually have ?

Fish fingers !

Where would you find a pilot whale ?

On board a flying fish !

★

Two men were walking along in the desert.
One said to the other "This is a lovely sandy beach."
The other replied "Yes, but
the tide is a heck of
a long way out !"

"Goody," said a shark as a surfer sped by on the crest of a wave, "I love fast food!"

Did you know that fish mums and dads teach their children not to start eating maggots – in case they get hooked!

Why don't fish play tennis?

Because they always get caught up in the net!

What toys do baby fish play with?

Doll – fins!

What fish can make your feet light up?

An electric eel!

What do fish do for adventure ?

They scale mountains !

What sort of fish go to heaven when they die ?

Angel fish !

How do vampire fish communicate ?

With wails !

Roses are red,
violets are pink,
there's an octopus in
the bath, so I'll get
washed in the sink !

What do you give a deaf fish ?

A herring aid !

Why do you suck your maggots before putting them on the hook ?

So I can wait for the fish with baited breath !

What do fish do when the TV breaks down ?

Send for the electric eel !

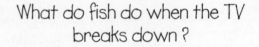

Which sea creatures do you need for a game of chess ?

Prawns !

Which fish like to dance in long lines ?

Conga eels !

What do sharks eat for tea ?

Fisherman's fingers and chips !

What do chip shops
on other planets sell?

**Fish and
computer chips!**

★

What do fish parents give their
children at Easter?

Oyster eggs!

★

Knock, knock...
Who's there?
Kipper...
Kipper who?
**Kipper your mouth shut, I don't want
anyone to know I'm here!**

★

Hey, Cod, you couldn't loan
me a fiver could you?

**What about the twenty
squid you already owe me?!**

What sort of fish never
have any money ?

Poor - poises !

What sort of music do
dolphins prefer ?

Sole music !

What sort of fish can you train to fetch your paper
every morning ?

A Dogfish !

What sort of fish likes
to work fingers to
the bone ?

Piranha Fish !

What do sharks call people who fall off speedboats?

Fast food!

Why don't sharks eat people in submarines?

They don't like tinned food!

Why are fishmongers so unpleasant?

Because their job makes them sell fish!

What is the best way to get a message to a fish?

Drop it a line!

631

Who was the most notorious cowboy fish ?

Billy the Squid !

Why are fish
frightened of maths
teachers ?

**Because they are
good anglers !**

Why was the kipper sent
to jail ?

Because he was gill - ty !

How do fish like their crisps ?

Ready sea salted !

What do fish
watch on TV ?

**One foot in
the wave !**

★

Where do fish sleep ?

On a sea-bed !

What sort of trout can you see after a
thunderstorm ?

A Rainbow !

What did the Eskimo sing at suppertime ?

" Whale Meat Again..."

What did the mum whale say to the cry-baby whale ?

Stop blubbering !

What do sharks suck when they have a sore throat ?

A Fisherman's Friend !

What game do young
fish play at parties ?

Sardines !

What do fish watch on TV ?

Cod-roe-nation street !

What sort of fish is always getting
under your feet ?

An eel !

★

What do you give to a deaf sea nymph ?

A Mermaid !

Holiday Hoaxes

What do you call someone who casts spells
at the seaside ?

A Sandwitch !

When we went on holiday last year - the aeroplane was so old...

...it had solid tyres !

...the 2 previous owners were the Wright Brothers !

...one of the seats said "Reserved for Julius Caesar" !

...the co-pilot had to keep running to the tail to rewind the motor !

...the seats were covered in dinosaur hide !

...the pilot was taught to fly by Baron Von Richtofen !

Who always gets the sack after his first day at work ?

Father Christmas !

Dear Santa...

If I'm good
it's understood
that you'll bring me
a new CD.

If I'm kind
I know I'll find
a guitar to play
on Christmas Day.

So from now on,
You're going to find,
that I'll be helpful,
good and kind,
and I intend to
stay that way!
At least, that is,
'til Boxing day!

★

Where do Santa's workers go when they
are sick?

The National Elf Service!

What do you call two girls with Christmas
decorations on their heads ?

Holly and Ivy !

Where do snowmen go to dance ?

Snowballs !

Our maths teacher is going
to the Caribbean this *Summer* !

Jamaica ?

No, she wanted to go !

We stayed in a really posh hotel on our
holiday last year - it was so posh that
the number for room service
was ex-directory!

Waiter! This egg is bad!

That's not my fault. I only laid the table!

How do fish go on holiday?

By octobus!

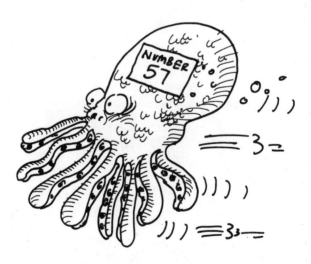

What sort of clothes do people wear
in very hot countries ?

Blazers !

Where are the Andes ?

On the ends of your armies !

Why do birds fly South in the Winter ?

It's too far to walk !

When bees go on holiday where do
they wait for the coach ?

At a buzz stop !

What is grey, has four legs and a trunk ?

A mouse going on holiday !

Why did the elephant wear sunglasses on the beach ?

Because he didn't want to be recognised !

A witch wanted to go on a motor cycling holiday...

...so she bought abrrooommm stick !

"Good morning ladies and gentlemen. Welcome aboard the World's first ever fully computerised aeroplane. There is no need for a pilot or co-pilot on this aircraft, as everything is fully automated. We are currently flying at 30,000 feet and everything is working perfectly...working porfectly...burking lurfectly...smirking carpetly..."

What flavour crisps can you use to take you on holiday ?

Plane !

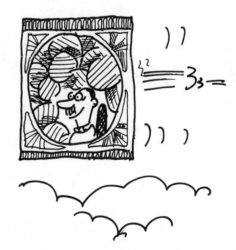

Where do school dinner ladies go on holiday ?

Greece !

Why do policemen like to go to
discos when they are on holiday ?

They really enjoy the beat !

What's big and grey and flies you to
your holiday destination ?

A jumbo jet !

Three friends went on a cruise holiday, but were
shipwrecked on a desert island. A good fairy came
and gave them one wish each. The first two men
wished they were back at home with their families.
The third man thought for a minute and said, "It's
quiet around here all on my own, I wish my two friends
were still here with me !"

Waiter - do you have frog's legs ?

Yes, monsieur !

Well, hop into the kitchen and get me a steak !

★

Tourist-Do you have a room for the night ?

Hotelier-Certainly, sir. £40 a night or £10 a night if you make your own bed.

Tourist - I'll take the £10 room please !

Hotelier - Fine. You'll find the wood in the room and I'll bring the hammer and nails up in a minute !

★

What do jelly babies travel
in on holiday ?

A jelly copter !

★

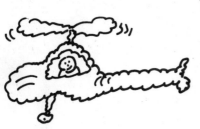

Where do monks go for a break ?

Holy-Day camps !

Two friends had enjoyed a great days
fishing on a lake.

*"We must come here again," said one,
"but how will we ever find this same spot
on such a huge lake?"*

**"No problem," said his friend, "I've marked
an X on the side of the boat !"**

What do cave men do on holiday ?

They go out night-clubbing !

How do cave men afford holidays ?

They club together !

Did you remember to bring the
sun-protection cream ?!

**Yes, but I would have thought the sun would
be used to the heat by now !**

★

Passenger - I'm nervous,
I've never flown before ?

Hostess - Oh, don't you
start, I've got enough
trouble with the pilot !

★

My holiday was in ruins this year !

I'm sorry to hear that !

Oh! it's OK - I went on an archaeological dig !

Dear Santa...

I've been good - really means - **I haven't broken any windows for a whole week now !**

I'm kind to dumb animals - really means - **I sometimes help my little brother with his homework !**

I help old ladies to cross the road - really means - **I dropped a bottle of cooking oil outside the old folks' home and they all skidded on it !**

I stay behind at school all the time to do extra work - really means - **I am constantly in detention !**

I look forward to receiving a little something from you in my Christmas stocking - really means - **Fill up the two duvet covers and three pillow cases with presents fat man or there'll be trouble !!**

What do movie directors put on their
Christmas cakes?

Starzipan!

Why are you eating all those
tins of baked beans?

**I'm going windsurfing this
afternoon!**

Where does a vampire go to see
the illuminations?

Dracpool!

What do you call a reggae singer who
looks after chairs on the beach?

Desmond Deckchair!

Where does a monster sleep on a
camping holiday ?

In a sleeping bog !

Which holiday camp do vampires prefer ?

Batlins !

What do people wear on their heads
in very cold countries ?

Ice caps !

Where do jockeys spend their holidays ?

Horse - tria !

Where do birds go for a holiday ?

Coven - tree !

What is grey, has four legs and 2 trunks ?

An elephant going on holiday !

Why did the cow use sun tan oil ?

Because she didn't want to tan her hide !

Why did the witch go to France ?

Because she fancied a spell abroad !

How do footballers go on holiday ?

By coach !

How do cavemen get to their holiday destinations ?

They fly club class !

Why do monsters put people in their suitcases ?

They like to take a packed lunch !

What do monsters like to eat best on holiday ?

Beaches and cream !

Tourist - Can I have breakfast in bed ?

Hotelier - **Of course, but most of our guests find a plate more sensible ?!**

Stupid Sports

What was the name of that brilliant
Russian billiards player ?

Inoff the Red !

What job does Dracula have with the
Transylvanian cricket team?

He looks after the bats!

Sporting Booklist...

How to win at sport

by

Vic Tree

Horse training

by

Jim Kana

The cricketers' quiz book

by

R.U. Stumped

How can you describe cricket in three words ?

Rain Stopped Play !

★

What do you call the cat playing football ?

Puss in boots !

★

My cousin has gold and silver medals in Karate, Cricket, Snooker, Horse Riding, High Jump, 200 Metres, Swimming, Marathon and Javelin !

Wow - he must be a super athlete !

No - he's a burglar actually !

Why has the groundsman
covered the grass in tar !?

**Well – you told him to lay the
pitch out for tonight's match !**

My Barry's in the Olympic Archers team you know !

Goodness – he must be a
super shot ?

**No, he's rubbish, but he's
heard every episode of
the Archers!**

Why are your hands covered in blood ?

Because I've just been giving a foot massage to our
Olympic team !

That's not usually a dangerous
thing to do is it ?

**Only when they forget to take their spiked running
shoes off !**

I knew Kevin was an underachiever when he had his Olympic gold medal bronze-plated !

What do you call a spooky cricketer ?

A wicked keeper !

It was a terrible tragedy, one of the World's finest sprinters - died from pneumonia !

Look on the bright side - at least his nose kept running until the very end !

We'll never finish this bowling match !

What makes you say that ?

Well - every time I knock all the pins down, someone calls everyone out on strike !

What did it say on the snooker player's gravestone ?

Farewell to Jim, who has taken the long rest !

There was a time when he would get through 3 or 4 marathons a week - but he's not touched one for months now !

Why is that ?

Well - they changed the name to Snickers !

Odds & Ends

Why are you taking that shovel to your
singing class ?

So I can get to the low notes !

What do you call an underwater spy ?

James Pond !

What sort of dancing will elephants
do in your front room ?

Break dancing !

Knock, knock...
Who's there ?
Boo.
Boo who ?

No need to get upset, it's just a game !

Where would you find a rubber trumpet?

In an elastic band!

What time is it when you have
eaten half of your lunch?

Half ate!

Doctor, doctor...
I feel like the man in the moon!

What has come over you?

A cow!

What sort of car is a Rolls-Canardly ?

A car that rolls down hills
but can hardly get up them !

What is a duck filled fatty puss ?

An overweight cat that has just eaten a duck !

How do electricians get over high fences ?

They volt !

I asked for vegetarian sausage -
these are made from beef !

But the cow was a vegetarian !

Where does Father Christmas go
for his Summer holidays ?

Santa Maria !

Hello, Carol, how was your first day at school ?

First - you mean I have to go back again ?!

Did you hear about the cowboy who used to sit up all
night making models of cows from tissue paper - he
was sacked for rustling !

A man ran into a bar and got three fractured ribs...

...it was a steel bar !

A man wanted to be a lumberjack...
He flew out to Canada and bought
a chainsaw and got a job.
At the end of the first week he
had cut down 100 trees.
'That's not enough,' said the foreman,
'we expect you to cut down at least 200.'
However, he offered to buy the man's
chainsaw to help with his air fare home.
"I'll just test it first,' said the foreman,
and started the engine.
**'How do you get it to make that noise?'
said the man !?**

What do ghosts shout at a bad play ?

Booooooooooo !

What do skeletons say after they've
seen a really good play ?

That was a rattling good show !

How does Jack Frost get about ?

By Icycle !

What do you call a travel agent in the jungle ?

A Trip - opotamus !

What drink do Australian bears manufacture ?

Coca - Koala !

Which animal tells the best jokes ?

A stand -up chameleon !

What's the quickest way to get out of the jungle ?

By ele - copter !

Why do wolves howl at the moon ?

Because they have such rotten singing voices !

My Dad must be the greatest magician ever -
yesterday he turned his car into a side street, and the
day before he turned it into a lay-by !

Waiter - where's my elephant sandwich ?

Sorry, Sir, I forgot !

What do bogey men drink ?

Demon - ade !

Who do female ghouls get married to ?

Edible batchelors !

What prize is awarded each year to the best dieter ?

The No - Belly Prize !

Nurse - can you take this patient's temperature please ?

Certainly doctor - where to ?

Why are you taking that shovel to your singing class ?

So I can get to the low notes !

Before you give anyone a piece of your mind -
check to make sure you will have enough
left for yourself afterwards !

What's round, shiny, smelly and comes out at night ?

A foul moon !

Does Cyclops get a television licence at half price ?

Are my indicators working ?

On and off !

Why is that farmer setting fire
to the plants in his field ?

He's growing baked beans !

Why did you give up your job as a fortune teller ?

To be honest I couldn't see any future in it !

How do you know if a Boa-constrictor loves you ?

It will have a crush on you !

Why do boxers like going to parties ?

They love to get to the punch !

How do you know where an
escaped train is hiding ?

Just follow the tracks !

What sort of boats do clever
schoolchildren travel on ?

Scholar - ships !

Who runs the pub in the jungle ?

The wine-ocerous !

Knock, knock...
Who's there ?
Alison.
Alison who ?
Alison to you asking me that question every day !

Knock, knock...
Who's there ?
Alpaca.
Alpaca who ?
Alpaca suitcase and leave if you keep
asking these silly questions !

What do you get if the central heating goes haywire in a pet shop ?

Hot dogs !

What game do prisoners like best ?

Cricket - they like to hit and run !

Which vegetable is best at snooker ?

The Cue - cumber !

What do you call a man who preserves pears ?

Noah !

What did the artists say when he had to choose a pencil ?

2B or not 2B, that is the question !

We're going to build a bonfire,
put our maths books on the top,
put school dinners in the middle,
and burn the bloomin lot !

Why did the stick insect cover himself
with marmite ?

**He was going to a fancy dress party
as a twiglet !**

Which ancient leader invented
the cruet set ?

Sultan pepper !

Is that bacon I smell ?

It is and *you* do !

What is a robot's favourite snack ?

Nucler fission Microchips !

What do you do with a ladder in
a hot country ?

Climate !

What goes up a drainpipe down but
can't come down a drainpipe up ?

An Umbrella !

What animal lives on your head ?

The hare !

Did you hear about the robot policeman ?

He was a PC - PC !

And - did you hear about the mechanical writer ?

Robot Louis Stevenson !

Where do monsters go fishing ?

Goole !

Why did the idiot try to spread a goat on his toast ?

Because someone told him it was a butter !

Where should you send a one-legged,
short sighted man ?

To the hoptician !

What do you get if you cross a bird with a frog ?

Pigeon toed !

What did the paper say to the pencil ?

You lead me astray !

Doctor, are you sure it's my arteries that
are the problem ?

Listen I'm a doctor, aorta know !

When is a King like a book?

When he has lots of pages!

★

Why did the jelly wobble?

Because it saw the milk shake!

★

Water – A colourless liquid that turns brown
when you put your hands into it!

★

Why did the idiots stand in an open doorway?

They wanted to play draughts!

Why didn't the idiot's home-made airbag stop him from breaking his nose when he crashed?

He didn't have enough time to blow it up!

Where do very tough posties sleep?

On pillow boxes!

Why were the judge and jury on a boat?

Because the prisoner was in the dock!

What sort of food is made from old Chinese boats?

Junk food!

Why are so many famous artists French?

Because they were born in France!

What do you call a happy crcodilewith a camera?

Snap happy!

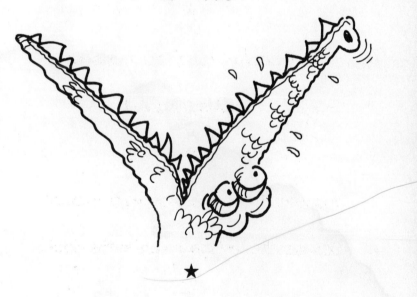

Why did the American Indian chief put smokeless fuel on the fire?

He wanted to send some secret messages!

Did you hear about the man who drove round telling everyone he was rich and successful, when he was actually a failure ?

He was a mobile phoney !

Why was the poor dog chasing his tail ?

He was trying to make ends meet !

How do you know when you come to the end of a joke book ?

Because there's no more laughing matter !

Joe - Last night I opened the door
in my pyjamas !

**Jim - Why on earth have you got a door in your
pyjamas ?**

What do you call a bird drinking two drinks
at once ?

Toucan !

Did you hear about the monster who ate
a settee and two chairs for lunch ?

He had a three piece suite tooth !

Mum, can you help me with my maths homework, I'm
trying to find the lowest common denominator ?

**Crickey, they were trying to find that
when I was at school !**

What do you get if you cross
a pig with a dinosaur?

Jurassic Pork !

When the monster had finished his tea he
asked his mum if he could leave the table.

**She said yes he could, as long as
he had eaten the chairs !**

KEEEAAA!!!

Waiter, why is this
chop so tough?

It's a Karate chop, sir !

Which snake tells tales?

The grass snake !

How do you stop a mouse from squeaking?

Oil it!

Which two kings were good at fractions?

Richard the third and Henry the eighth!

Who was the first man on the moon?

A spaceman!

What lies under your bed at night with its tongue hanging out?

Your shoe!

Why was the cat lying on the toast rack?

It was a marmalade cat!

What would happen to a penguin
in the desert?

The chocolate would melt!

Have you heard about the boy who kept
a pencil in his bedroom...

**...so he could draw the curtains
every morning!**

Little Miss Muffet
sat on a tuffet,
eating tandoori and rice.
A monster from Bury
ate Miss Muffet and curry,
and said 'by golly that was nice!'

Joe -Which is the best side to have
the handle of a teacup on?

Jim - The outside !

★

I would tell you the joke about quicksand...

...but it might take a while to sink in !

★

I wish you wouldn't cheat
when we play cards !

How do you know I'm cheating ?

Because you're not playing
the hand I dealt you !

What do you do with a red monster ?

Take it back to the library and
get another one to read !

What is a good parting gift ?

A comb !

What did the Pink Panther say when he
stood on an ant ?

Dead Ant, Dead Ant,
Dead Ant Dead Ant Dead Ant
Dead Ant Dead Ant...

How do ducks play tennis ?

They use a tennis quack-it !

Why did the cannibal go to the wedding ?

**Because he heard they were going
to toast the bride and groom !**

★

Hostess – does this aeroplane travel
faster than the speed of sound

No Madam !

Good, because my husband and I want to talk !

★

What is the longest night ?

A fortnight !

★

Booklist...

The complete gardener

by

Rosa Cabbage

How to combat stiffness

by

Arthur Ritus

The Sandwich Makers Book

by

Roland Butter

The Titanic Story

by

I.C. Water

Operator, can you put me
through to the zoo ?

Sorry, the lion is engaged !

What can you tell me about the Dead Sea ?

Crikey, I didn't even know it was sick !

How do you flatten a spook ?

Use a spirit level !

Why were you breaking the speed limit ?

I was trying to get home before
my petrol ran out !

Teacher - I wish you would pay
a little attention Blenkinsop !

Pupil - I'm paying as little as I can !

★

What is the best time to pick apples ?

When the farmer is away on holiday !

★

Where were all the Kings
and Queens of France
crowned ?

On the head !

★

How does a woman know
when she has fallen in love
with a cricket player ?

**She is completely bowled
over !**

Spell a hungry bee in
three letters !

M T B !

Why did the sprinter run across everyone sitting
in the park ?

Because his trainer told him to run over twenty laps !

How do you make a cat happy ?

Send it to the Canary Isles !

Who is Postman Pat's favourite actor ?

Terence Stamp !

Why was the baby goat a crazy mixed up kid ?

Because he fell into the spin dryer !

What do you call a prisoner's budgie ?

A jail bird !

When are you allowed to take toffee to school ?

On a chews day !

Why do doctors
hate teachers
when they come
to see them ?

Because they never
give them enough
time to do the
examination !

Knock Knock...
Who's there ?
Scot...
Scot who ?
Scot nothing to do with you !

★

Knock Knock...
Who's there ?
Cher...
Cher who ?
Cher this orange with me - it's too big
for me to eat on my own!

History teacher -
Can anyone tell me what a forum is ?

Blenkinsop -
A two-um plus a two-um sir ?!

Pupil - What is this ?

Dinner attendant - It's bean soup !

Pupil - **Maybe - but what is it NOW !**

Why are teachers welcome in snooker halls ?

Because they always bring their own chalk !

Where do teachers get all their information ?

From Fact - ories !

Knock Knock...
Who's there ?
Bob...
Bob who ?
**Bob down and I'll pass your letters
through the catflap !**

★

What boat can cats sail ?

A catamaran !

What goes *moo, moo*, splash !?

A cow falling into the sea !

★

What does a
mouse say when
you take his photograph?

CHEESE!

★

Why do monsters not mind
being eaten by kindly
ghosts?

**Because they know they
will always be in good
spirits!**

★

What do monsters fasten
their
suitcases to the car roof-
rack with?

Franken - twine!

★

What does Dracula tow
behind his car on holiday ?

A Caravanpire !

★

My parents think you're great...really means...

...They think someone as weird as you
will put me off boys/girls for the next 10 years !

★

Well, Mr. Blenkinsop, your cough sounds much better this
morning !

So it should, doctor, I've been up
all night practising !

Who brings Christmas presents
to werewolves?

Santa Claws!

HO
HO
HO!

★

Doctor, doctor, my wife thinks
I'm a hypochondriac!

Why haven't you been to see me before about this?

I've been too ill!

★

Doctor, doctor, I think I'm a dog!

Well, take a seat and I'll have a look at you!

I can't - I'm not allowed on the furniture!

★

What do you get if you cross a frog and a fizzy drink?

Croaka - cola!

★

Doctor, doctor, I think I will have to give up jogging!

Why?

Because whenever I stop my nose keeps running!

What do you get if you cross a fruit and a woman who needs help?

A damson in distress!

What do you get if you train a reindeer to be a hairdresser?

Styling Mousse!

Wow, it's hot in this stadium, I'm boiling!

Well, come and stand next to me - I'm a fan!

Why are you putting that apple
in the rowing boat ?

You told me to put the cox in !?

★

"One hundred and eighty !"

I'm new to darts - is that a good score ?

Score ? - That's his waist measurement !!

What is a vampire's favourite sport ?

Point to point ?

Who serves the meals on a spooky aeroplane ?

The Air Ghostess !

What do you call a German barber ?

Herr Dresser !

Did you hear about the man who went
to the doctor and told him he
thought he was a piano ?

The doctor gave him a note !

What do you get if you cross a pig
with a hedgehog ?

A porkupine !

Why do teddy bears never hear what you say ?

Because they have cloth ears !

Doctor, doctor, I feel like a bird!

Well, you've come to the right place for tweetment!

What sort of fish flies a spaceship?

A Pilot Whale!

What do you call a wobbly book full of telephone numbers?

A jellyphone directory!

Our games teacher once tried to swim
across the English channel !

Did he do it ?

No - he got halfway across and had to turn
back because he was so tired !

Music teacher - Why are you standing
on that chair ?

Pupil - So I can reach the high notes !